QuickClicks
REFERENCE GUIDE

MICROSOFT®

OUTLOOK 2010®

QuickClicks Outlook 2010 Reference Guide

1st Edition

Litho U.S.A.

Distributed in the U.S. and Canada

For orders or more information, please contact our customer service department at 1-800-556-3009.

ISBN: 978-1-60959-044-4

Item # 32014

Trademarks

Disclaimer

The QuickClicks Reference Guide series is dedicated to all of CareerTrack's devoted customers. Our customers' commitment to continuing education and professional development inspired the creation of the award-winning *Unlocking the Secrets* CD-ROM series and the *QuickClicks Reference Guide* series.

Thank you for your continued support!

Contents

contents

Introduction

Congratulations on your purchase of *QuickClicks: Outlook 2010*. You have invested wisely in yourself and taken a step forward with regard to your personal and professional development.

This reference guide is an important tool in your productivity toolbox. By effectively using the email and task functions within Outlook, you will be able to maximize your efficiency. The powerful calendar and contacts tools will keep you and your most important asset – your connection to other people – organized. The tips in this reference guide are written for the user who has a basic understanding of word processing and at least one year of experience using other Microsoft Office applications.

Anatomy of a Tip

Each tip displays the tip title in the top left corner and the tip category on the top right, so you always know where you are and what you are learning. Each tip is written in plain English to help you find what you are looking for. Where appropriate, the tips include "What Microsoft Calls It" references so you can learn the lingo and perform more effective searches for additional feature capabilities in Microsoft's help system.

Each tip is assigned a difficulty value from one to four, with one circle representing the easiest tips and four circles representing the hardest.

Difficulty: ⭕⭕⭕⭕

All tips begin with a business scenario, identified as **PROBLEM**.

SOLUTION explains how the demonstrated feature might be used to solve the problem. A set of easy-to-understand instructions follows.

Letter callouts, **A**, point to important parts of the screen. The names of all selections and buttons are bolded and easy to find

Extras Include the Following

Icon	Name	What It Means
	Bright Idea	Bright Ideas offer suggestions for how the feature just demonstrated can be further used in an everyday setting.
	Hot Tip	Hot Tips share related functions and features, or additional uses of the features and functions, with the one being demonstrated.
	Caution	Cautions draw attention to situations where you might find yourself tripped up by a particularly complicated operation, instances when making an incorrect choice will cause you more work to correct, or times when very similar options might be confusing.

There are two other bonuses that do not have miniature icons. They are displayed at the end of tips, where appropriate. These are:

Icon	Name	What It Means
	Options	Options represent places where there are two or more ways to accomplish a task, or where two or more results might be obtainable, depending on the choices you make. Option icons appear within the text, and all relevant choices are next to the icon.
	Quickest Click	Quickest Clicks indicate there is a quicker way to accomplish the same task taught in the tip. Shortcuts like this, though, may leave out important steps that help you understand what you are doing. Because of this, each tip teaches the most complete method for accomplishing a task, and a Quickest Click appears if there is a quicker option.

At the bottom of each page, you will see either a Continue or a Stop icon. These icons indicate whether a tip continues on the next page or if it is complete.

Getting Around Outlook 2010

Items Seen in the Outlook Window

Microsoft Outlook works similarly to most other Microsoft Office 2010 applications in terms of window structure and basic function. Outlook offers four different task views: Mail, Calendar, Contacts, and Tasks. The modules and panes displayed in each view can be customized for that task. You can display the Navigation Pane in Normal size in the Mail View and set it to Minimized in the Calendar View, for example. Change between views in the Navigation Pane. Customize your View on the View Tab.

The Outlook Window

A **File Tab**

Click this button to access the Backstage View and locate New, Open, Save, Print, and other Outlook options.

B **Quick Access Toolbar**

Place items here for quick and easy access. The Save button is a default tool in the Quick Access toolbar. Click this button when you need to save your Outlook project.

C **Title Bar**

Displays the View you are in and any other relevant information such as which email account or folder you are looking at.

D **Ribbon/Tabs/ Groups**

Locate Outlook menu items and controls.

E **Reading Pane**

This is where your messages, contact cards, tasks, and appointments are displayed.

F **Navigation Pane**

Navigate between Mail, Calendar, Contacts, Tasks, or Notes View. the pane displays folders within the view you have selected.

G **To-Do Bar**

Displays your Calendar, To-Do List, and Appointments. Add and update tasks.

H **People Pane**

View contact information, recent interactions, and social media updates from the person associated with the activity you are viewing.

I **Navigation Buttons**

Click these to quickly move between Outlook Views. You can customize selection and order of the buttons on the Navigation Pane.

J **Zoom Slider**

Zoom is the display size of a slide within the slide window. A higher zoom percentage (300%) makes everything appear larger, while a lower zoom percentage (50%) makes everything smaller. Use the plus and minus buttons to increase and decrease zoom.

K **View Shortcut Buttons**

Click to select pre-set view shortcuts for each Task View.

L **Help Button**

Click this to open Microsoft Outlook's Help Search Window.

M **Search Box**

Type a keyword or contact name to return messages, appointment, contacts, and task results that match your search phrase.

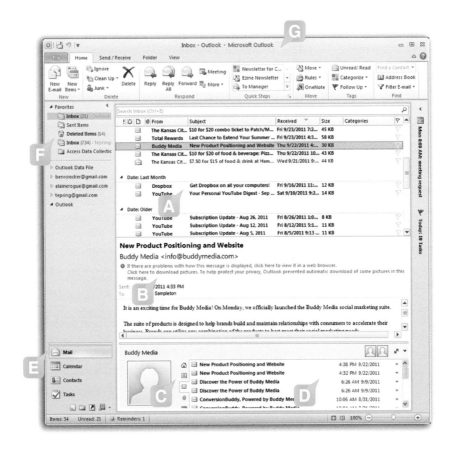

Mail View

A	**Reading Pane**	View your list of email messages. Double-click on any message to open it in a new window.
B	**Preview Pane**	View the content of a message you have selected without having to open it in a new window.
C **D**	**People Pane, Email Tab**	View contact information, recent interactions, and social media updates from the person associated with the activity you are viewing. Click the email Tab **D** to view all recent emails sent to or received from the person whose message you are viewing.
E	**Mail Button**	Click this to open Mail View.
F	**Mail Folders**	In Mail View, the Navigation Pane will display your email folders and subfolders.
G	**Title Bar**	In Mail View the Title Bar will reflect which folder and email account you are currently viewing.

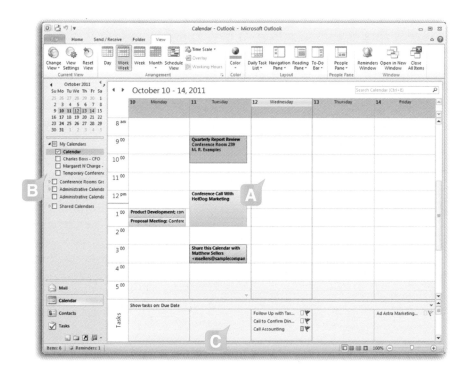

Calendar View

A **Reading Pane**
View your appointments on an interactive calendar. Choose arrangement options to sort your dates by Day, Week, and Month, or use Schedule View to compare shared calendars.

B **Calendar Folders**
In Calendar View, the Navigation Pane will display the calendars and calendar groups you have created.

C **Daily Task List**
View the tasks associated with the dates you are looking at. You can update task status and categorize tasks in this pane.

Contacts View

A Contacts

View your Contacts and their information. Choose arrangement options to view your contacts in List, Business Card, or Contact Card format. Sort and filter your contacts to find the information you are looking for.

B Reading Pane

View the selected contact's detailed information.

C Contact Folders

In Contacts View, the Navigation Pane will display the Contacts folders and sub-folders that you have created.

D People Pane (Minimized)

Expand to view contact information, recent interactions, and social media updates from the person associated with the activity you are viewing.

E Electronic Business Card

See contact's information displayed in business card format. This is what you will see when you attach and email an e-business card from your contacts list.

F Contact Photo

You can add a photo of your contact to their contact card.

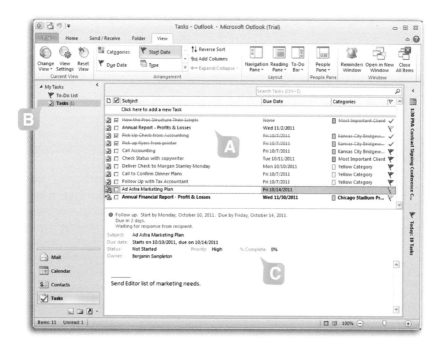

Tasks View

A **Tasks or To-Do List** — View your tasks. Choose arrangement options to sort your tasks by Due Dates, Category, Subject, Flag Status, etc.

B **Reading Pane** — See task details for the item you have selected.

C **Task Folders** — Choose between Task View and To-Do List View. The To-Do list includes Outlook Items that you have flagged for follow-up; such as email messages and contacts. The Task View only shows Items you have specifically created as a task.

Items You'll See on the Ribbon

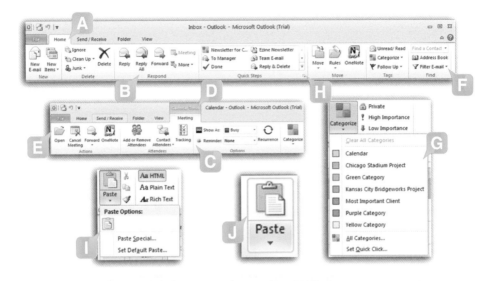

Items You'll See on the Ribbon

A Tab
Collections of related features and functions.

B Group
Collections of related controls.

C Highlighted Ribbon Section
Contextual ribbon sections that appear when some objects are selected or used.

D Contextual Tabs
Some specialized tabs only appear when a particular feature is active. These special tabs usually appear in conjunction with a highlighted ribbon section.

E Button
Single-click controls that perform one function.

F Dropdown Menus and Dropdown Buttons
Some buttons have a graphic and a down-pointing arrow, while others have a default selection visible, followed by a down arrow. Clicking the arrow reveals additional choices.

G Selection Box
A panel containing a list of selectable items.

H Panel Launcher or More Button
A scroll control that can be clicked to launch a selection panel.

I Dialog Box Launcher
A special group control that launches a related dialog box.

J Combo Button
These controls are split into two parts to function as both a button and a dropdown. They may be split horizontally or vertically.

Note: The Ribbon changes depending on your screen size, window size, and resolution. A small window might display only icons on the Ribbon ██, whereas a large window might display the full text for each button or open a selection box ██ . The images shown in this book might look different from what you see on your own screen. However, icons will always remain consistent and the group names and placements will be the same (unless you have customized your Ribbon).

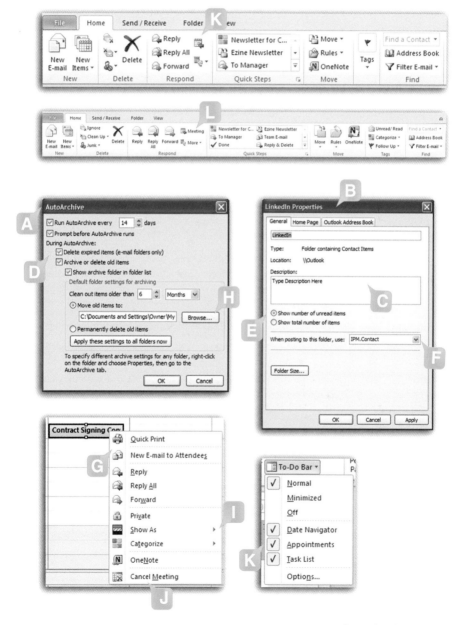

Items You'll See in Menus and Dialog Boxes

A Dialog Box
A feature-specific box that you can launch to control various functions in Excel.

B Tabs
Some dialog boxes have tabs similar to the one on the ribbon. Each tab is focused on a particular subset of features.

C Textbox
A box where text can be typed.

D Checkbox
A box that activates the related selection when checked and deactivates it when unchecked. More than one checkbox may be checked in a series.

E Radio Button
A circle that activates the related selection when selected and deactivates it when deselected. Only one radio button may be selected in a series.

F Dropdown View
A simple down-pointing arrow button that reveals a set of selectable choices.

G Right-Click Menu
This two-part menu appears when you right-click anywhere on the sheet.

H Dialog Box Launcher
In menus, buttons that launch dialog boxes are followed by ellipses (...).

I Menu Launcher
Menu selections that open additional menus are followed by right-pointing arrows.

J Shortcut Keys
Menu selections that can be launched by a keystroke on your keyboard are identified by the underlined letters in them. Click any underlined letter in a menu to launch that selection's function.

K Toggle Checkmarks
Some menus have checkmarks. Clicking an unchecked item in those lists checks it and activates the selected option. Clicking a checked item unchecks it and deactivates the selected option.

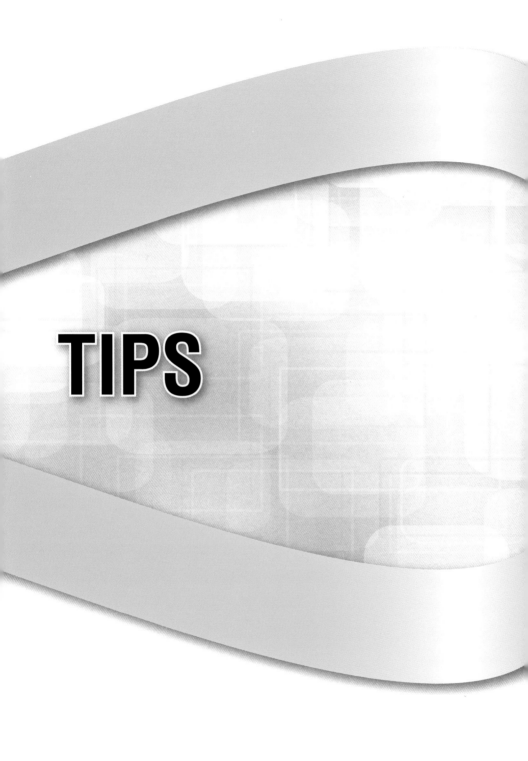

TIPS

1 Microsoft Outlook Email View

The following section will help you send and manage your email messages. Outlook gives you many tools to customize your messages as you create them. It offers just as many tools for organizing and reading your messages so you can organize not only your inbox, but also your time more efficiently.

The following tips will all refer to the Mail View unless otherwise noted. To make sure your Outlook window is in the Mail View, check to see if the Mail View button **A** is selected at the bottom of the Navigation Pane.

If you do not see the Navigation Pane on the left side of your Outlook window, you may need to open it. Click the Navigation Pane button **B** in the Layout group on the View tab and then select Normal or Minimized **C** from the dropdown menu.

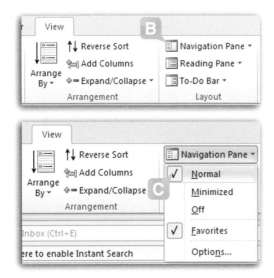

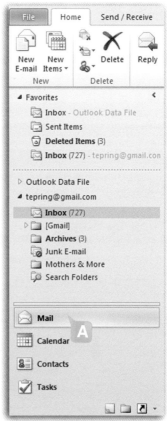

1 Create a New Email Message

Difficulty: ○○○○

PROBLEM You need to send a follow-up email to your co-worker after your meeting today about the new project.

SOLUTION Prepare a new email. Outlook is a powerful communication tool that helps you send clear and informative messages in the most efficient way possible. Messages can be as simple as a few lines of text or as detailed as an HTML brochure. Email can be used for many tasks, from assigning work to scheduling appointments to catching up with a friend. When you open a new email window, you are opening a conversation.

Step-by-Step

1. On the **Home** tab, click the **New Email** button A in the **New** group to open a new message window.

2. Type in the email address of the recipient in the **To…** text box B.

3. Type a brief description of your message in the **Subject:** text box C.

4. Type your message in the **message window** D.

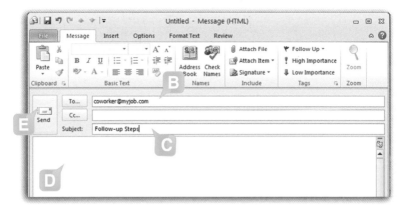

5. When your message is ready to send, click the **Send** button .

 Quickest Click: When you type an address into the **To...** line, Outlook 2010 Auto-Complete will offer you email addresses that are similar to the one you are typing .
- To select a name from the Auto-Complete List, click the name that you want entered into the **To...** text box, or press the **ENTER** or **TAB** key.
- To ignore an Auto-Complete option, simply keep typing the address.
- To delete a name from the Auto-Complete List so that you will not be offered that name again, click the **X** next to the name .

Hot Tip: To look up and enter an email address from your address book, click the **To...** button 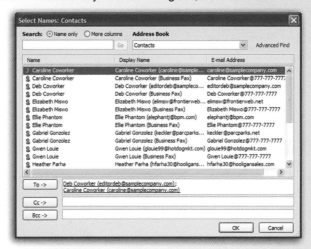 to open the **Select Names** dialog box. Choose or search for the contacts your email will go to, then click **OK**.

2 | Create a Personalized Signature

Difficulty: ○○○○

PROBLEM You are a lawyer just opening your own firm, and you want to put your new contact information and a confidentiality notice at the bottom of every email. The contact information includes your name, title, company, phone, email, and website. You want to add all this information without having to type it every single time you write an email.

SOLUTION Creating an email signature will automatically attach your personal contact information to all emails that you send. By adding an email signature you can effortlessly give co-workers, employees, clients, etc., the information they need to contact you.

See Also: Create A New Email Message

Step-by-Step

Create a Signature File

1. Open a new message.

2. In the message window, click the **Signature** button A in the **Include** group on the **Message** tab.

3. Select **Signatures** B to open the **Signatures and Stationery** dialog box.

4. Click the **New** button C.

5. Type a name for your signature in the **New Signature** text box D. Click **OK**.

6. Type the text you want to include in the signature in the **Edit signature** text box E. Change the font, size, and formatting of your text using the style and formatting buttons above the text box F.

7. When your signature is finished, click **OK**.

Step-by-Step

Insert a Signature into an Email Message

1. Open an email message window. Place your cursor in the message pane where you want your signature to appear.

2. Click the **Signature** button A in the **Include** group on the **Message** tab.

3. Select the signature file G you want to include from the dropdown menu. The signature will appear in the message pane H.

Hot Tip: If you want your signature added to every email you send, you can tell Outlook to insert the signature automatically. Click the **Signatures** option under the **Signature** button to open the **Signatures and Stationery** dialog box.

Choose default signature

E-mail account: tepring@gmail.com

New messages: External Communication Signature

Replies/forwards: (none)

Under the **Choose default signature** heading, select the email account associated with the signature, then select the signature file you want attached to every new message from the **New messages** dropdown menu . Click **OK** to close the dialog box and save your settings. All new messages will open with the signature already inserted.

Choose **(none)** if you do not want Outlook to add a signature automatically to your new messages.

Bright Idea: Use the **Insert Picture**, **Insert Hyperlink**, and **Insert Business Card** links  above the **Edit signature** text box to add value and visual appeal.

Edit signature

Calibri (Body) 11 **B** *I* U Automatic Business Card

Confidentiality Notice: The information contained in this e-mail message and any attachments thereto is attorney-

3 Attach a File to Your Message

Difficulty: ○○○○

PROBLEM You have a .PDF file of a new product proposal that your marketing department has created. You need to send the proposal to your boss, who is in Chicago.

SOLUTION The easiest way to do this is to attach your .PDF file to an email message addressed to your boss. Once your document has been attached, sending the email will include the attached file along with your message. The attachments feature allows you to send any document in any electronic format offering you an easy way to share important information.

Step-by-Step

1. Open a new message. When you are ready to attach a document, click the **Attach File** button **A** in the **Include** group on the **Message** tab to open the **Insert File** dialog box.

2. Browse to and select the document you want attached to your message **B**. ⚠

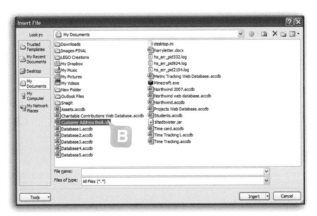

3. Click **Insert**. The document's name will appear in the **Attached:** box in your message window.

4. Finish typing your message, then click **Send** D.

Caution: All mail servers have message size limits that may prevent a message from being delivered if your attachment's file size is too big. Many email accounts also have storage limits. A very large document may fill your recipient's mailbox or exceed their storage limits and get "bounced," i.e., returned undelivered to you.

Be aware of these size limits and watch for returned messages if a file you are sending happens to be very large. You can also look for ways to reduce the size of very large messages by compressing pictures and other media, or by compressing the entire document with a compression format such as .zip.

4 Change Your Default Email Settings

Difficulty: ○○○○

PROBLEM Your insurance agency has many customers with older email programs that don't display HTML messages correctly. You want to use Rich Text Format when sending your emails instead of HTML so all your clients can read your messages. You are also annoyed by the sound you hear every time a new email arrives, especially when you have customers meeting with you in your office. You would like a way to make these preferences the default for all your messages instead of changing them each time you open a new message.

SOLUTION Change your email default options. The Options tab in the File menu allows you to change everything from your message notification tone to font styles to themes, etc. Once you define your preferences in the Outlook Options dialog box, Outlook will remember those preferences each time you open it.

Step-by-Step

1. Click on the **File** tab A, then click the **Options** button B to open the **Outlook Options** dialog box.

2. Click the **Mail** tab C to see the settings options for email messages you create and receive:

- **Compose messages:** Under this heading, you can create signature files, set default fonts and text colors for new messages, and specify how spellchecking and auto-correct function. To change all new messages to the Rich Text Format instead of HTML, choose **Rich Text** from the **Compose messages in this format:** dropdown menu 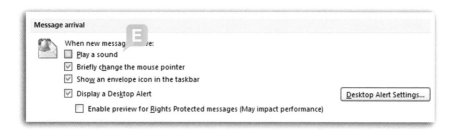.

- **Outlook panes:** Change how received messages are identified as **read** or **unread**.
- **Message arrival:** Customize how your desktop responds when you receive a new message. You can customize notice features (such as how a Desktop Alert will look) or turn them off completely. To set your Outlook so that no sounds are played when new messages arrive, click the **Play a sound** checkbox to uncheck it.

- **Conversation Clean Up:** Under this heading, you can customize how the **Clean Up** feature will affect messages in your folders. You can choose which folders items will be moved into, which messages are allowed to be moved (unread, flagged, categorized, etc.,) and how **Clean Up** will affect replies.

- **Replies and forwards:** Customize how your message looks when replying or forwarding email. You can choose to indent the original author's text in the same message or append it to the message as an attachment. You can specify text to preface all new text and tell Outlook how to handle replies in a plain-text message.

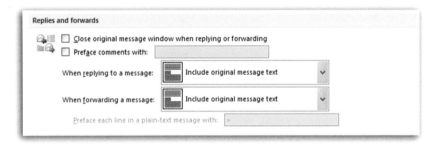

- **Save messages:** Specify how and when messages are saved as drafts. Allows you to turn off the feature that saves messages into the **Sent Items** folder.

- **Send messages:** Under this heading, you can specify the default **Importance** or **Sensitivity** level of a new message and turn off features such as Automatic name checking, Auto-Complete, and the **CTRL + ENTER** shortcut key. You can also set new messages to expire after a specified number of days.

- **Tracking:** Set tracking and delivery instructions that will apply to every new message.

- **Message format:** Customize how your messages are formatted and encoded and specify default text wrapping preferences for every new message.

- **Other:** Customize Outlook behaviors such as shading message headers and where your window returns when you have completed a task.

5 | Create a New Folder and Move Emails into That Folder

Difficulty: ◯◯◯◯

PROBLEM As an architect for a small firm, you usually work on three or more separate projects at any given time. You want a way to organize your email so you can easily find messages relating to a given project without digging through all of your unrelated emails.

SOLUTION Create email folders. By creating separate folders to organize emails by different subjects, you can cut down on the time you would normally exhaust looking through your inbox. With separate folders, each project and its associated messages are easily accessed without having to search through unrelated email.

Step-by-Step

Create an Email Folder

1. Click the **Folder** tab , then click the **New Folder** button B in the **New** group to open the **Create New Folder** dialog box. ⚡

2. Select the folder in the **Select where to place the folder:** pane C under which you want your new folder to appear.

3. Type a name for your new folder in the **Name:** text box D.

4. Click **OK**. Your new folder will now appear E in the **Navigation Page** as a sub-folder of the existing folder you selected.

Step-by-Step

Add Email to a Folder

Option 1 - Drag and Drop

1. Make sure the **Navigation Pane** is open. To open the navigation pane, click on the **View** tab, then click the **Navigation Pane** dropdown button **F** in the **Layout** group. Select **Normal** **G** from the dropdown menu.

2. Click and hold down the mouse button over the email you want to move **H**, then drag it over the folder where it should go. Your cursor will display a small envelope **I** to show that you are moving an object.

3. When the correct folder is highlighted, release the mouse button. Your message will move into the folder **J**.

4. Click on the folder in the **Navigation Pane** to view your messages **K**.

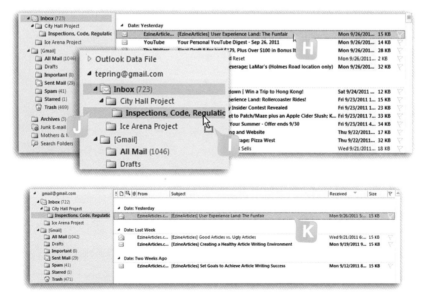

Option 2 – Right-Click

1. Right-click on any message in the message pane to open the fly-out menu.

2. Hover over the **Move** menu option to open the **Move** fly-out menu.

3. Click on the folder you want the message to move into . 🔥

4. Click on the folder in the **Navigation Pane** to view your messages .

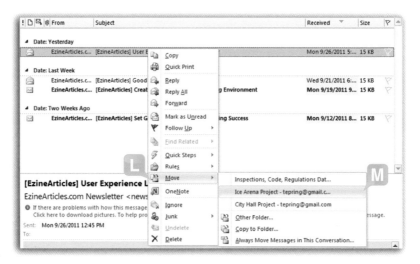

Quickest Click: To quickly create a sub-folder, right-click on any folder in the **Navigation Pane** and then select **New Folder**  from the fly-out menu.

Hot Tip: If you want to file duplicate messages into more than one folder, select **Copy to Folder**  instead of the folder name from the **Move** options menu. Select the destination for your copied message in the **Copy Items** dialog box, then click **OK**. Your message will appear in *both* folders.

6 Add Voting and Tracking Options to an Email

Difficulty: ○○○○

PROBLEM You want to get a quick answer to see who will be attending your HR department's Lunch & Learn training at 12:30 tomorrow afternoon so you can order the correct number of box lunches. You also want to follow up by phone with anyone who has not RSVP'd. It would be helpful to know who has and has not read your email.

SOLUTION Microsoft Outlook allows you to add a voting function to your emails, which will give your recipients the opportunity to choose an answer from a number of options that you provide. Enable **Tracking Options** to see when your recipients open your email. Once the recipients interact with their message, you can view the results of your poll and quickly identify those who have opened your email.

Note: A Microsoft Exchange Server account is required for this feature to function fully. If your recipients do not use Outlook or are not on an Exchange server, they may not be able to participate in your poll, and you may not be able to receive tracking information accurately.

See Also: Create A New Email Message

 **Step-by-Step**

Add a Poll to Your Email

1. Open a new message.

2. Click the **Options** tab , then click the **Use Voting Buttons** dropdown button ⃣.

3. Select the option you want for your voting button names. In our example above, you would want a definite Yes or No, so select the **Yes;No** option ⃣. To create custom names for your voting buttons, choose **Custom** ⃣ from the dropdown menu to open the **Properties** dialog box.

Under the **Voting and Tracking options** heading, check the **Use voting buttons:** checkbox 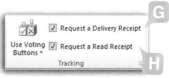. Either choose your voting button names from the dropdown or click in the textbox and type your own button names. Each choice must be separated by a semi-colon.

4. To turn on tracking, click the **Request a Read Receipt** checkbox in the **Tracking** group on the **Options** tab to have Outlook inform you when a message is opened by the recipient. Click the **Request a Delivery Receipt** checkbox to have Outlook inform you when a message has been delivered (but not necessarily read).

Step-by-Step

Respond to a Vote Request

1. If a message you have received contains a poll, the header will say: **Vote by clicking Vote in the Respond group above.** To cast your vote in the poll, click the **Vote** button , then choose from the options in the dropdown menu .

2. To send your vote without any reply or comments, click the **Send the response now** radio button . To add a reply to your response, click the **Edit the response before sending** radio button. This will open a reply email window for you to edit and send as usual. Click **OK**.

Step-by-Step

View Your Voting Results

1. When a recipient replies to your poll, you will receive an email message with their choice displayed in the subject line **M**. You will also receive a **Read** reply email if you requested **Read** tracking **N**.

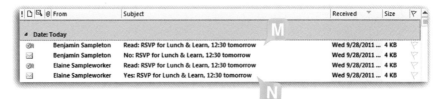

Open the Reply email message to see any comments they may have added. You will also see their voting result on:

- The **Subject:** line **O**
- The message bar **P**.

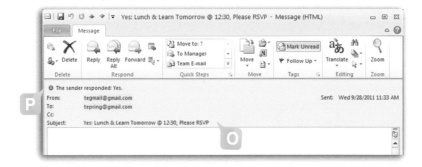

Bright Idea: If you send lots of polls or tracking requests, your inbox may get very cluttered with replies, making it hard to find and sort the results. Set up a Rules filter to automatically sort your replies into folders for quick access. *See also: Create and Manage Rules*

 Quickest Click: To quickly see a report of responses to your poll, right-click on the information bar in a message window or in the reading pane, and then click **View voting responses** Q.

7 Modify Delivery Date and Reply Settings

Difficulty: ◯◯◯◯

PROBLEM You are sending out an e-mail to request nominations for the "Employee of the Month." You do not want people to start the nominations until Friday, but you will be out of the office till next week. You also want everyone to reply to your assistant so she can tabulate the results.

SOLUTION Use the **Delay Delivery** option to hold all of your outgoing emails in your outbox until the time that you specify. You also have the ability to use the **Direct Replies To** button to enter your assistant's email address so that all replies are sent to her.

See Also: Create A New Email Message

Step-by-Step

Specify When Your Message Will Be Delivered

1. Open a new message.

2. Click on the **Options** tab, then click the **Delay Delivery** button  in the **More Options** group to open the **Properties** dialog box.

3. Under the **Delivery options** heading, check the **Do not deliver before:** checkbox B. Type in or use the dropdown calendar to set the date you want your message delivered C. Type in or use the dropdown date to set the time of day your message should be delivered D.

4. Click **Close** when you have completed your changes.

Step-by-Step

Specify Who Will Receive Replies

1. Follow the directions above to open the **Properties** dialog box.

2. Check the **Have replies sent to:** checkbox **E** under the **Delivery options** heading.

3. Type in the name of the person whom you want to receive message replies into the text box, or click the **Select Names…** button and choose a name from your contact list. Separate multiple names in the textbox with semicolons.

4. Click **Close** to apply your changes.

5. Click **Send** to complete the message.

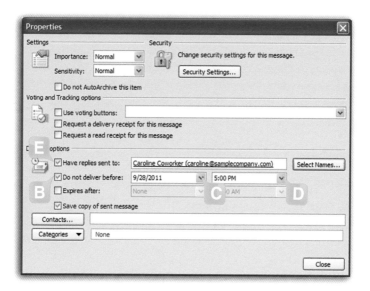

8 | Filter Junk Mail out of Your Inbox

Difficulty: ◯◯◯◯

PROBLEM You are getting a lot of junk mail in your inbox, which makes it hard to find important messages among the clutter. You are also spending a lot of a time sorting and deleting the junk mail. You would like a way to get rid of the unwanted emails without having to handle each individual message.

SOLUTION Enable the Junk Email Filter option to direct all undesired messages to a separate folder. The Junk Email Filter will sort your email automatically, allowing the messages from your contacts to arrive in your inbox and filtering out messages that qualify as junk mail.

Outlook's Junk Email Filter evaluates whether a message is spam based on several factors such as when the email was sent, who sent it, and the content of the message. The default protection level for the Junk filter is **Low**, but you can change this to filter more aggressively. Email that is filtered by the Junk Email Filter is not deleted; it is moved to the Junk Email folder where you can view the messages if needed.

There are several ways you can tell Outlook which emails you want and which ones you consider junk. To make sure that messages from regular or important senders appear in your inbox, you can add them to your **Safe Senders** or **Safe Recipients** lists. To filter specific addresses or senders, you can add them to your **Blocked Senders** lists. Using a combination of these techniques will reduce the clutter in your mailbox and save you valuable time.

Step-by-Step

Change Your Junk Email Protection Level

1. On the **Home** tab, click the **Junk** dropdown button  in the **Delete** group.

2. Select **Junk Email Options**  to open the **Junk Email Options** dialog box.

3. On the **Options** tab in the **Junk Email Options** dialog box, select the radio button beside the level of protection you want:

    • **No Automatic Filtering:** This setting will turn off the Junk Email automatic Filter, but domain names and addresses that you have manually blocked on your **Blocked Senders List** will still be removed from your inbox.

    • **Low:** Use the Low setting if you don't receive much junk mail. This filter will remove only the most obvious spam messages.

    • **High:** If you receive a lot of junk mail, you may want to choose the High setting to aggressively filter messages from your inbox. Even though all senders on your safe lists will be approved, you should regularly review your messages in the Junk Email folder when using this setting.

    • **Safe Lists Only:** All email is classified as junk unless is sent from an address on your Safe Senders List or from a mailing list on your Safe Recipients List. This is the most restrictive filter. You must regularly review your messages in the Junk Email folder if you choose this setting.

4. Click **OK** to apply your new settings.

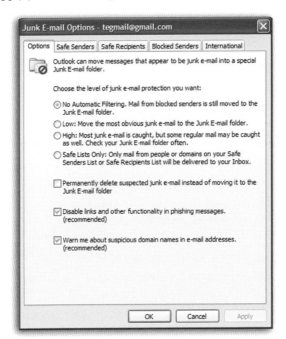

Step-by-Step

Add addresses to your Safe Senders, Safe Recipients, and Blocked Senders Lists

1. To add an e-address or domain name to any of the Junk Email Filter lists, select a message **A** from the sender you want to protect or block, then click the **Junk** button **B** in the **Delete** group on the **Home** tab.

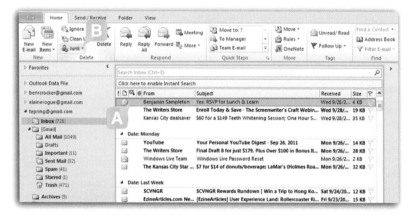

2. Choose an option from the pulldown menu:

- **Block Sender:** Messages from addresses or domains in the **Blocked Senders List** are always treated as junk. New messages received from this sender will automatically be sent to the **Junk Email** folder, regardless of content.

- **Never Block Sender:** Adds the sender to your **Safe Senders List.** Messages received from this specific person will never be considered junk.

- **Never Block Sender's Domain:** Adds the domain name of the sender you have selected to the **Safe Senders List**. Use this feature when you communicate with several from the same company, for example, so you don't have to add each individual separately to your safe list.

- **Never Block this Group or Mailing List:** Since an email mailing list forwards messages from many different participants, it can be impossible to add every member to your safe list. Choosing this setting tells Outlook that all messages sent through the mailing list are safe without having to add individual addresses.

3. Click **OK** to acknowledge your selection 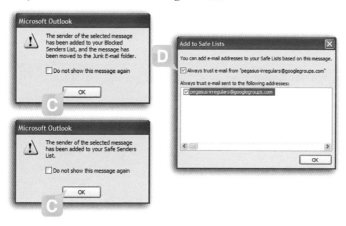, or click the check-box beside the addresses you want to add in the dialog box , and then click **OK**.

4. To view the addresses on your Blocked Sender and Safe Sender lists, click the **Junk** button in the **Delete** group on the **Home** tab, then select **Junk Email Options...** to open the dialog box.

   - Click on the **Safe Senders** tab to view the list of addresses that have been added to your safe senders list.

   - Click on the **Safe Recipients** tab to view the list of address that are on your safe recipients list.

   - Click on the **Blocked Senders** tab to view the list of addresses that you have blocked.

   - Click on the **International** tab to view addresses you have blocked based on country code or language.

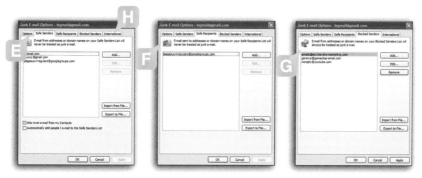

Step-by-Step

Retrieve Messages from the Junk Email Folder

1. To view messages that Outlook has considered junk, click on the **Junk Email** folder  in your **Navigation Pane**.

2. Select the message that you do not wish Outlook to consider spam and then click the **Junk** button.

3. Choose **Not Junk** 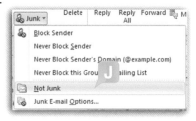 from the dropdown menu.

4. If you wish to add the sender of the message to your safe sender list so future messages will not be sent to the junk folder, check the box beside **Always trust email from "address"** .

5. Click **OK**.

Bright Idea: It is likely that when you send an email message to someone, you will not want their reply or future messages to be considered junk. You can tell Outlook to add everyone with whom you communicate to your safe senders list automatically, saving you the trouble of adding people manually.

In the **Junk Email Options** dialog box, on the **Safe Senders** tab, check the **Automatically add people I email to the Safe Senders List** checkbox to tell Outlook to turn on this feature.

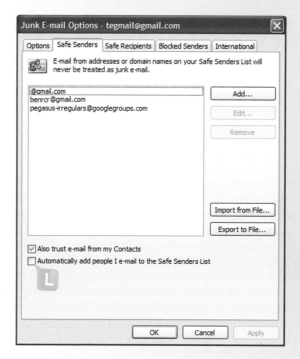

9 Clean Clutter out of Your Inbox

Difficulty: ◯◯◯◯

You are no longer a part of the office party committee, but they haven't removed you from their list, and your inbox is filled with email updates that you are not interested in.

The **Ignore Conversation** feature conveniently allows you to select a specific set of emails that you wish to have automatically removed from your inbox. The **Conversation Clean Up** tool reduces clutter by deleting messages that contain redundant content.

A conversation, or email thread, is a set of messages that share the same subject line. A conversation consists of an initial email through all of its replies and responses. A conversation can be many messages long, with many different people responding to parts of the content.

Each time a message is replied to, the previous content is included in the reply, in essence duplicating each message every time a new message is sent. When a conversation gets long, your inbox can get crowded with messages that essentially contain multiple copies of the same content. **Conversation Clean Up** evaluates the contents of each message and deletes old messages that are duplicated in more recent messages, allowing you to reduce clutter without losing information.

Sometimes you will be included in a group conversation that you no longer have any interest in reading. In this case, you can use Outlook's **Ignore Conversation** feature to automatically delete all future messages associated with that subject line. Because the Ignore feature is based on conversations, rather than sender, you can block specific topics without blocking all messages from a sender you regularly communicate with.

Step-by-Step

View Your Inbox by Conversation

1. To sort your messages by conversations, click the **View** tab, then put a check in the **Show as Conversations** checkbox  in the **Conversations** group.

2. In the dialog box, click the **All folders** button  to apply this grouping in all folders in your mailbox, or **This folder** to apply this grouping only to the folder you are currently working in.

Your grouped messages will appear in the message pane with an expand button to show or hide the individual messages associated with a subject title.

![Step-by-Step] **Step-by-Step**

Remove Redundant Messages

1. To initiate the **Clean Up** feature, click the **Clean Up** button in the **Delete** group on the **Home** tab.

2. Choose the conversations you want Outlook to review from the dropdown menu:

   • **Clean Up Conversation:** Only messages in the conversation you are currently viewing will be affected.

   • **Clean Up Folder:** All messages in the selected folder will be affected.

   • **Clean Up Folder & Subfolders:** All messages in the selected folder *and* its subfolders will be affected.

3. Click the **Clean Up** button in the **Clean Up Conversation** dialog box to apply the changes and move affected messages into the delete folder.

Step-by-Step

Ignore a Conversation

1. Select the conversation you no longer want to read .

2. Click the **Ignore** button 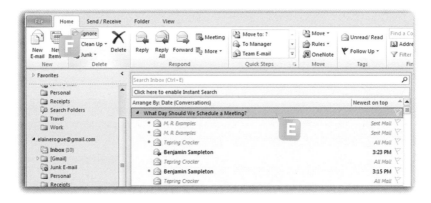 in the **Delete** group on the **Home** tab.

3. Click **OK**, then click **Ignore Conversation**  to apply the filter and send all future messages to the **Trash**.

Caution: Any automated filter that delete messages should be approached with caution. You can customize your **Clean Up** settings from the **Outlook Options** dialog box under the **File** tab. Microsoft recommends that you keep the **When a reply modifies a message, don't move the original** checkbox  active so that you will not miss any changes made to a previous reply.

10 | Send an Out of Office Reply

Difficulty: ⭕⭕⭕⭕

PROBLEM You are going on vacation for the week, and you want those who send you emails to know that you will not be able to get back to them right away.

SOLUTION Set an **Automatic Reply** while you are away. Any coworker or client who sends you an email while you are gone will receive your automatic reply. You can customize your reply to contain alternate contact information or a personal message regarding your absence.

Option: The steps for creating an out of office reply are different depending on whether you are on a Microsoft Exchange Server or not. Follow the steps that apply to the type of email account you are using.

Option 1: Out of Office Replies without an Exchange Server Account

See Also: Create A New Email Message

Step-by-Step

1. Open a new message.

2. Type the message that you want your contacts to receive when they email you while you are away.

3. Click the **File** tab **A**, then click **Save As** **B** to open the **Save As** dialog box.

4. Select **Outlook Template (*.oft)** **C** from the **Save as type:** dropdown menu.

5. Type a name for your out-of-office template message in the **File name:** text box **D**, then click **Save**.

6. In your main window, click the **Rules** button **E** in the **Move** group on the **Home** tab, and then select **Manage Rules & Alerts** from the dropdown menu to open the **Rules and Alerts** dialog box.

7. Click the **New Rule** button  on the **Email Rules** tab to open the **Rules Wizard**.

8. Under the **Start from a blank rule** heading, select **Apply rule on message I receive** , then click **Next**.

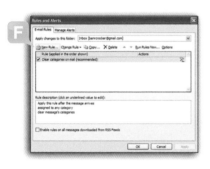

9. Select any further criteria you want your out-of-office reply to meet from the **Which conditions(s) do you want to check?** pane . Generally, if you simply want all messages to receive the out-of-office reply, you will not add conditions. Click **Next**. If Outlook prompts you with a **This rule will be applied to every message you receive. Is this correct?,** click **Yes**.

10. Under **What do you want to do with the message?** Heading, select **reply using a specific template** check box .

11. Under **Step 2: Edit the rule description (click on an undefined value)**, click **a specific template** to open the **Select a Reply Template** dialog box.

12. In the **Look In:** dropdown menu, select **User Templates in File System** . Browse to the folder where you saved your out-of-office templace and select it , then click **Open**. The filename and path will appear in the **Step 2** pane. Click **Next**.

13. Select any exceptions you want your auto-reply rule to consider from the **Are there any exceptions?** pane M. Generally, if you want all messages to receive the out of office reply, you will not add exceptions. Click **Next**.

14. Type a name for your out-of-office reply rule in the **Step 1: Specify a name for this rule** text box N.

15. Click **Finish** to apply the new rule. ▲

Caution: For an auto-reply rule to send replies automatically through an email account that is not a Microsoft Exchange Server email account (such as a POP3, IMAP, or Windows Live Hotmail account) Outlook *must be running* and configured to periodically check for new messages from your email server.

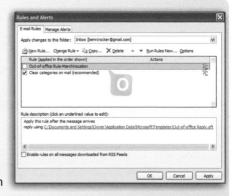

Caution: You must also remember to turn off your auto-reply rule when you no longer need the auto-replies sent. To turn off your rule, click the **Rule** button in the **Move** group on the **Home** tab, and then select **Manage Rules & Alerts**. Under the **Rule** heading, un-check the check box for the rule that you want to turn off O.

Option 2: Out of Office Replies Using an Exchange Server Account

Step-by-Step

1. Click the **File** tab , then click the **Automatic Replies** button B on the **Info** tab to open the **Automatic Replies** dialog box.

2. Click the **Send Out of Office auto-replies** radio button C to turn on the auto-reply feature.

3. To set a date and time range for the auto-reply to be active, click the **Only send during this time range:** checkbox D, and then specify a **Start time:** and **End time:** in the dropdown menus.

4. You can create different responses to messages received from within your organization and those received from outside your company. You can also set the auto-reply to respond only to one or the other. Click the **Inside My Organization** tab or **Outside My Organization** to write your response for those messages. Check the **Auto-reply to** checkbox E to turn on replies for that tab.

5. Type your response message in the message pane F.

6. Click **OK** to save your messages and activate the auto-reply feature.

11 Microsoft Outlook Contacts View

The following section will help you create and manage your contacts. Whether you are simply storing email addresses or gathering detailed information about companies, organizations, and individuals, Outlook Contacts gives you many tools to organize and retrieve your data in a quick, efficient manner.

The following tips will all refer to the Contacts View unless otherwise noted. To make sure your Outlook window is in the Contacts View, check to see if the Contacts View button A is selected at the bottom of the Navigation Pane.

If you do not see the Navigation Pane on the left side of your Outlook window, you may need to open it. Click the Navigation Pane button B in the Layout group on the View tab and then select Normal or Minimized C from the dropdown menu.

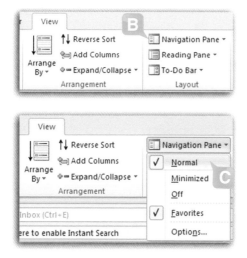

11 | Create and Update a Contact

Difficulty: ◉○○○

PROBLEM You just got a call from a new prospective client, and you want to make sure to save all her information so you can contact her later.

SOLUTION Creating a contact is an easy way to save a client's, co-worker's, employee's, etc., personal information so that you have ready access to it when you need it later. You can save anything from a simple name and phone number to multiple addresses, photographs, and business cards for your contact.

Option: There are several ways you may come across information you want to save in Outlook Contacts. Outlook not only lets you type in information from scratch, but it also can pull in contact information you may already be looking at, such as from an email message or an Electronic Business Card. Choose the option that will help you most quickly create a new contact.

See Also: Create a New Email Message

Option 1: Create a New Contact from Scratch

**Step-by-Step**

1. On the **Home** tab, click the **New Contact** button  in the **New** group to open a new contact window.

2. Type the name of your contact in the **Display as:** text box **B**. Fill in other information, such as company name and job title, in the name section. 🔥

3. Type the email address of your new contact in the **Email** text box **C**, or select from an Auto-Fill choice.

    To enter multiple email addresses for the same person, click the down arrow **D** next to the **Email...** button and choose **Email 2** or **Email 3**, then fill in the text box. Fill in any other information you have under the **Internet** heading.

4. Enter Phone numbers for your contact under the **Phone numbers** heading . The default phone categories that will appear on a new contact window are **Business**, **Home**, **Business Fax**, and **Mobile**. To change the category, or choose from more options, click on any phone category down arrow . Select up to four categories  to appear in the **Phone numbers** section.

CONTINUE

5. Enter an address for your contact in the text box under the **Addresses** heading . To enter multiple addresses for the same person, click the down arrow next to the default **Business** button and choose **Home** or **Other**, then fill in the text box. The address for the previous category will not be erased. Click the **Address** button again to switch between your address choices.

   If you have multiple addresses for a contact, select the one that any mailings you send should go to by checking the **This is the mailing address** checkbox.

6. Click the **Details** button in the **Show** group to access more categories of information.

7. Click the **Save & Close** button in the **Actions** group on the **Contact** tab to save your contact and return to the **Contacts View.**

Option 2: Create a New Contact from an Email

Step-by-Step

1. Open an email message from the person you want to add to your contact list.

2. Hover over the name of the person you want to add to your contact list until the pop-up **Contact Card**  appears.

3. Click on the **View more options** icon , then select **Add to Outlook Contacts** .

4. A **Contact** window will open with the name and email address already filled in .

5. Fill in any other information you want, then click **Save & Close**.

Option 3: Create a New Contact from an Electronic Business Card

Step-by-Step

1. Open the email message that contains an Electronic Business Card or .VCF file.

2. Right-click on the card and click **Add to Outlook Contacts** .

3. A **Contact** window will open with the information from the business card already filled in.

4. Fill in any other information you want, then click **Save & Close**.

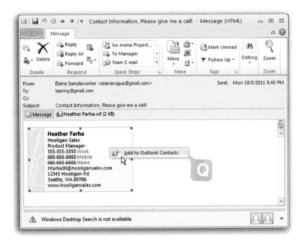

Caution: To avoid creating multiple contact cards for the same person, each with a slightly different set of data collected, Outlook will prompt you when it detects a duplicate entry. After you click **Save & Close**, if you see the **Duplicate Contact Detected** dialog box, you can choose to:

- Merge the existing contact card with the data you have just added – Click the **Update information of selected Contact** radio button. Outlook will show you which old data will be written over by the new data in the **Changes to Selected Contact:** pane .
- Add new contact – **Click the Add new contact** to create two separate contact cards with the same Contact Name. This will prevent Outlook from overwriting the information of another contact who happens to have the same first and last name.

Bright Idea: Add a photograph of your contact to help you remember what they look like when planning for a meeting or a first-time face-to-face introduction. In the Contact window, simply click the default photo thumbnail to open the **Add Contact Picture** dialog box. Browse to the image of your contact, select it, and then click **OK**.

Quickest Click: If you are entering multiple contacts in a row, click the **Save & New** button in the **Actions** group on the **Contact** tab instead of **Save & Close.** This will save the information you are working on and open a new, blank contact form without having to click the **New Contact** button again. *See Also: Enter Multiple Contacts from the Same Company.*

12 | Enter Multiple Contacts from the Same Company

Difficulty: ⭘⭘⭘⭘

PROBLEM You just landed a new business client. You are now entering in all the new contacts from that company, but you don't want to have to type the same address for each new contact over and over.

SOLUTION Use the **Contact from the Same Company** option. When creating contact cards, you can tell Outlook to automatically fill in the information that is most likely the same if a contact is from the same company. Once you have entered the company name, address, phone number and, website for your first contact card, you can easily create many more contact cards without having to re-type the same thing.

See Also: Create and Update a Contact

Step-by-Step

1. Open a new contact window and fill out all the information for your first contact as described.

2. When you are ready to save, click the dropdown button beside the **Save & New** button A in the **Actions** group on the **Contact** tab.

3. Click **Contact from the Same Company** B. The information you are working on will be saved, and a new contact window will open with the company information already inserted C.

4. Fill out the new contact card and repeat this procedure until you have entered all the contacts that work at the same company. Click the **Save & Close** button on your last contact card.

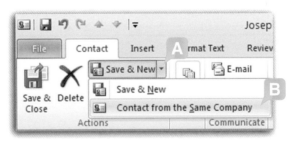

Original

Updated

13 | Forwarding a Contact

Difficulty: ○○○○

PROBLEM Your co-worker asks you if you have the phone number and address of the event planner you used for the awards banquet. You have the event planner in your contacts list, but you'd like a better way to give your co-worker the information without re-typing it once you have looked it up, or without copying and pasting every field from the contact window.

SOLUTION Forward the contact card as an attachment. Just as you can send a document as an attachment to an email, you can do the same with any of your saved contact cards.

Step-by-Step

1. Highlight the contact whose information you want to forward in the contacts pane **A**.

2. In the **Share** group on the **Home** tab, click the **Forward Contact** button **B**.

3. Choose how you would like the contact to be forwarded from the dropdown menu **C**:

   - **As a Business Card** - Outlook will open a new email message window with the contact card attached in .VCF format **D**. The business card will also be displayed in the message as a text card.

   - **As an Outlook Contact** - Outlook will open a new email message window with the contact card attached, your recipient will need to also use Outlook to make use of this file format. **E**

   - **Forward as Text Message** - Outlook has the option to send and receive mobile phone text messages. To use this feature, you will need to configure a text messaging account.

4. Add any other messages you want to include with the contact information, then click **Send**.

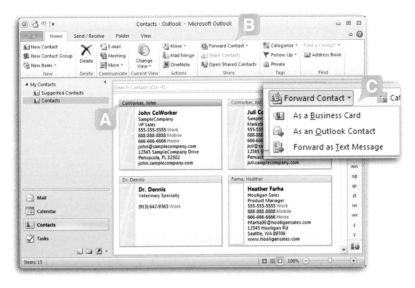

14 | Create a New Contacts Folder

Difficulty: ○○○○

PROBLEM You manage a small bakery and have many contacts, including clients who regularly order your cakes for corporate events and suppliers who provide you with your ingredients. It is getting hard to find the contacts you want within the jumble. You would like a way to separate your vendors' contact information from your clients.

SOLUTION Create a new **Contact Folder**. Outlook allows you to create as many contact folders as you need and to move contacts between these folders as you wish. Once you have your folders set up, you can easily keep your contacts organized.

Step-by-Step

1. Click the **Folder** tab **A**, then click the **New Folder** button **B** in the **New** group to open the **Create New Folder** dialog box. ✱

2. In the **Select where to place the folder:** pane **C**, select the folder under which you want your new folder to appear.

3. Type a name for your new folder in the **Name:** text box **D**.

4. Click **OK**. Your new folder will now appear **E** in the **Navigation Page** as a sub-folder of the existing folder you selected.

 Step-by-Step

Add Contacts to a Folder

Option 1 - Drag and Drop

1. Make sure the **Navigation Pane** is open. To open the **Navigation Pane**, click on the **View** tab, then click the **Navigation Pane** dropdown button **F** in the **Layout** group. Select **Normal** **G** from the dropdown menu.

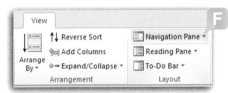

2. Click and hold down the mouse button over the contact card you want to move **H**, then drag it over the folder where it should go. Your cursor will display a small envelope **I** to show that you are moving an object.

3. When the correct folder is highlighted, release the mouse button. Your message will move into the folder **J**.

4. Click on the folder in the **Navigation Pane** to view your messages **K**.

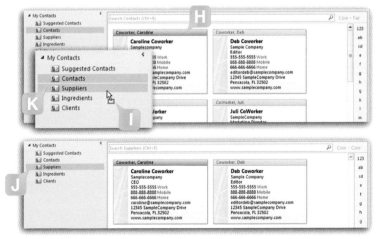

Option 2: Right-click

5. Right-click on any contact card in the contacts pane to open the fly-out menu.

6. Hover over the **Move** menu option to open the **Move** fly-out menu.

7. Click on the folder you want the contact to move into . 🔥

8. Click on the folder in the **Navigation Pane** to view your messages .

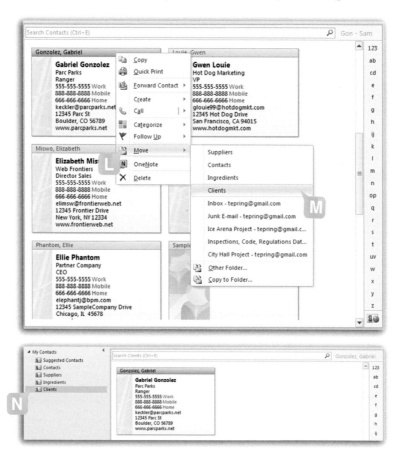

To quickly create a sub-folder, right-click on any folder in the **Navigation Pane** and select **New Folder**  from the fly-out menu.

Hot Tip: If you want to file duplicate messages in more than one folder, select **Copy to Folder** 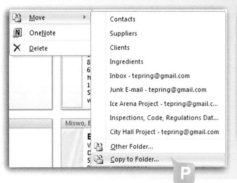 instead of the folder name from the **Move** options menu. Select the destination for your copied message in the **Copy Items** dialog box, then click **OK**. Your contact card will appear in *both* folders.

Caution: If you do copy a contact card, you must remember to update *both* cards when you make changes to that person's information. Otherwise, the contact information in one folder will remain out of date. Outlook does not automatically synchronize between copied contact cards.

15 | Create and Manage a Contact Group

Difficulty: ○○○○

PROBLEM You send a weekly report via email to your entire department. You want a way to send the report to the whole group without having to select each name individually each time.

SOLUTION Create a Contact Group. Microsoft Outlook allows you to send email to all the contacts you have associated with a specific contact group by typing only the group's name in the **To:** field. This feature was called **Distribution Lists** in previous versions of Outlook. There is no maximum to the number of names you can include in your groups, and individual contacts can be members of multiple groups.

See Also: Create an Email Folder; Create a Contact Folder; Create A New Email Message

Step-by-Step

Create and Add Members to a Contact Group

1. Click the **New Contact Group** button  in the **New** group on the **Home** tab to open a contact group window.

2. Type a name for the group in the **Name:** text box .

3. In the **Members** group, on the **Contact Group** tab, click the **Add Members** button .

4. Select the location of the person you would like to add to your group from the dropdown menu 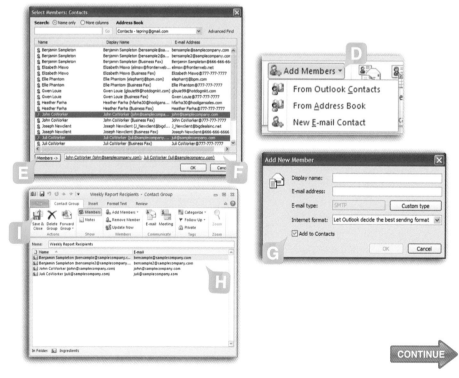D:

    • From **Outlook Contacts** and **From Address Book** – These selections will open the **Select Members: Contacts** dialog box. Select the person you want to add to your group, then click the **Members** button E to add the names to the **Members** text box F.

    SHIFT+Click to select a contiguous group of contacts, or **CTRL+click** to select multiple, individual contacts. ◊

    • **New Email Contact** – This selection will open the **Add New Member** dialog box. Fill out the contact information for the new contact, then click **OK**. To add this new contact to your Contacts list in addition to your group, check the **Add to Contacts** checkbox G.

5. Click **OK** to add the contact to your group. The names will appear in the **Members** pane H of your **Contact Group** window.

6. Click **Save & Close** I to create your group and save the members you have added to it.

CONTINUE

Step-by-Step

Manage Your Contact Groups

1. Contact Groups are, by default, filed with your contacts in the **Contacts** folder. To view and edit the contact group, double-click on the group in your contacts pane  to open the contact group window.

2. To add members to your group, click the **Add Members** button in the **Members** group and follow the steps above.

3. To remove a member from your group, select it on the members pane **K**, and then click the **Remove Member** button **L** or hit the **DELETE** key.

4. Click **Save & Close** after you have completed your changes.

5. To move your contact group into a different contacts folder, drag and drop the group into the folder where you want it to be filed.

Step-by-Step

Send Email to a Contact Group

1. Open a new email message.

2. Click the **To…** button **M** to open the **Select Names: Contacts** dialog box.

3. Select the name of your contact group **N** from the list, then click the **To>** button **O** to add the group to your **To:** line. Alternately, you can add groups and contacts to the **Cc:** and **Bcc:** lines of your message.

4. Click **OK**. The group name will appear in the **To:** text box ▣.

5. Type your message and add any attachments you wish to send to the group. Click **Send** to send the message to every name on the contact group list.

 Hot Tip: When you are adding people to your members list, find contact cards more quickly by using the address books and contact folders you have already created. In the **Address Book** dropdown menu ▣, select the folder or address book where your contact is located to to narrow the list in the contacts pane.

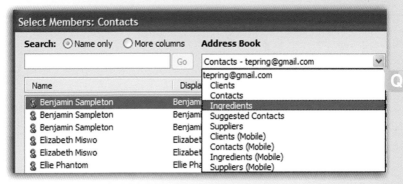

16

Send a Meeting Request to a Contact Group

Difficulty: ○○○○

PROBLEM You have just scheduled a department meeting for next Wednesday. You need to let everyone in your department know about it and you want to make sure it's in their calendars.

SOLUTION Just as Outlook allows you to send one email to all members of a contact group, you can also send a meeting request to a contact group.

See Also: Create and Manage a Contact Group; Schedule a Meeting

Step-by-Step

---

1. In the **Contact Pane**, double-click the **Contact Group** you wish to invite to your meeting to open the **Contact Group** window.

2. Click on the **Meeting** button **A** in the **Communicate** group on the **Contact Group** tab. A new meeting window will open with the contact group already inserted into the **To:** line **B**.

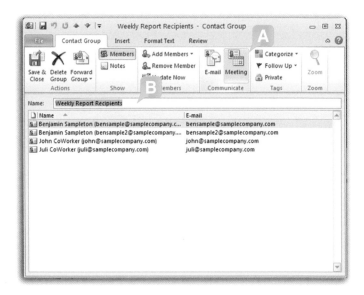

3. Fill in the topic and location of your meeting in the **Subject:** and **Location:** textboxes.

4. Specify the meeting's **Start time** and **End time** by selecting the date and time from the pulldown menus. If the meeting will be an all-day event, click the **All day event** checkbox .

5. In the **Message** pane , type your message with details about the meeting or instructions to the group who will be attending.

6. When your invitation is complete, click **Send**. All members of your contact group will receive the meeting invitation.

17 | Add a User Defined Field

Difficulty: ○○○○

PROBLEM As HR director at a small manufacturing company, you need to collect Emergency Contact information, including names and phone numbers, for all your employees. You would like to store this information in your Outlook Contacts, but the default contact window doesn't have fields for the information you need.

SOLUTION Create a User Defined Field to customize contact data to your exact requirements. A User Defined Field will allow you to create your own text, numeric, memo, date, and other fields. You can then save this information to use at a later date in the format that is most useful.

 What Microsoft Calls It: Create a Custom Field

Step-by-Step

Create a User Defined Field

1. Open a contact window.

2. Click the **All Fields** button A in the **Show** group on the **Contact** tab.

3. Make sure that **User Defined Fields in this item** B is selected from the **Select from:** dropdown menu.

4. Click the **New** button C at the bottom of the window to open the **New Column** dialog box.

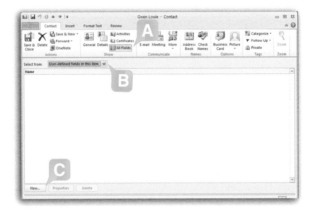

5. Type a name for your new field in the **Name:** text box .

6. Select the appropriate type for your field from the **Type:** dropdown list . Among the options included are:

   • **Text** – Field will be an empty text box for user to fill in.

   • **Number** – Field will prompt user for a numeric entry. Select the Format property you want for your numeric field in the **Format:** dropdown list . Choices include **All digits, Truncated, 1 and 2 Decimal, Scientific,** and **Computer**.

   • **Percent** – Field will display the entered value as a percentage. Format property choices include **All digits, Rounded, 1 and 2 Decimal**.

   • **Currency** – Field will display entered value in dollars.

   • **Yes/No** – Choose format properties from different yes/no options.

   • **Date/Time** – Choose the way you want the date displayed in the format properties.

7. Click **OK**. Your new field will appear in the **User-defined fields in this item** pane. Click in the **Value** column to type the relevant information into the field .

8. Click **Save & Close** to save your changes to the contact card.

CONTINUE

Step-by-Step

View User Defined Fields

Not all fields fit on the contact form in **Card** view. If your new fields do not appear on your contact form, you can always view them in the **All Fields** view under the **User-defined fields in folder** view. You can also add your new fields to the **List** view by following the steps below:

1. On the **View** tab, click the **Change View** button  and then select **List** view from the dropdown menu .

2. Click the **View Settings** button to open the **Advanced View Settings: List** dialog box.

3. Click the **Columns...** button to open the **Show Columns** dialog box.

4. To add your custom fields to the List view, choose **User defined fields in folder** from the **Select available columns from:** dropdown menu  to see your custom fields in the **Available columns:** pane.

5. Select the fields you want to see in List view, then click the **Add** button to move the fields into the **Show these columns in this order:** pane. Move the fields up or down the list by selecting them and clicking the **Move Up** or **Move Down** buttons.

6. Click **OK**, and then **OK** again to close the **Advanced View Settings List** and apply your view changes. Your custom fields will appear in List view where you placed them in the **Show Columns** dialog box.

18 | Create a Custom Electronic Business Card

Difficulty: ○○○○

PROBLEM A new prospective client gave you their business card. You want to enter all the information on the card, including a tagline and logo into their contact information so you can refer to it when you make your follow-up call. You would also like the electronic business card you send to contacts to look unique and impressive.

SOLUTION Outlook's Business Card view gives you a concise way to display a contact's most important information so you can reference it at a glance. Often, the information that your contact considers most important is already on the business card they have taken the time to create and print. If this card contains information that is not included in Outlook's default business card view, you can modify it to reflect the data you want to save.

Furthermore, you can customize your own business card to reflect your company's colors and fonts, and even include a logo to create an electronic business card that is just as visually appealing as your printed cards.

Step-by-Step

1. Open a contact window for the person whose business card you want to customize. This can be your own contact information if you want to design your own card.

2. Right-click on the **Business Card** [A] in the contact form pane and choose **Edit business card** [B] to open the **Edit Business Card** dialog box.

3. To change the lines of information that appear on the business card, click on a field name in the **Fields** pane C. Changes you make will be updated in the **preview pane** D. ⚠

- To move the field up or down on the card, select it and click the **Up** or **Down** arrows E.

- To remove a field from the business card, select the field to delete and click the **Remove** button F.

- To add a field, click the **Add...** button G and choose the field you want included from the dropdown menu.

- To specify whether your field will display a label (such as "Work" and "Mobile" for phone numbers), click on the **Label:** dropdown arrow H and choose from **No Label, Left,** or **Right**.

- Type in or change the text for a label in the **Label:** textbox I. You can even change the color of the label by clicking the **Label:** color button J. Choose the color you want for your label from the dialog box, then click **OK**.

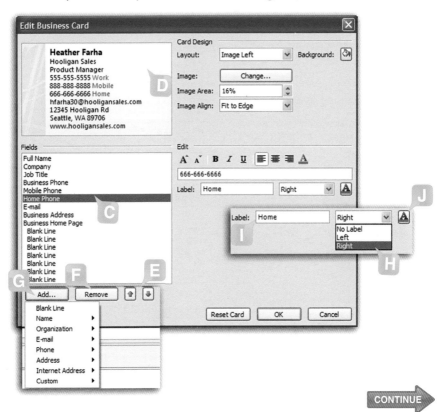

CONTINUE

Create a Custom Electronic Business Card   67

4. To change the formatting of the text in your business card, click on the field you want to change in the **Fields** pane and then make your formatting choices under the **Edit** heading . From here you can **increase** or **decrease** the font size, make your text **bold**, **italic**, or **underlined**, change the alignment to **left**, **right**, or **center**, and specify a custom **color** for your font.

5. To customize the background and layout of your business card or to add your own image, make your choices under the **Card Design** heading:

   • To change the background color, click on the **Background:** button **L**.

   • To add your own image to the business card, click the **Change...** button **M** to open the **Add a Card Picture** dialog box. Browse to and then select the image you want to use, then click **OK**.

   • To adjust where and how your image appears on the card, choose from the options in the **Layout:** dropdown menu **N**.

   • To specify how much space your image takes up on the card, use the **up and down arrows** on the **Image Area** option **O**.

   • Adjust your image's position in the **Image Align:** dropdown menu **P**.

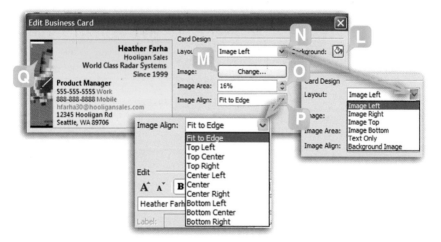

6. When you are satisfied with your custom business card, click **OK** to close the **Edit Business Card** dialog box. You will see your new business card in the contact form .

7. Click **Save & Close** to save your changes.

> **Caution:** Even if a field is available in the **Fields** pane of the **Edit Business Card** dialog box, you may not see it on your business card if there is not room to display it. Always check your preview pane to make sure the information you need is visible.

19 | Outlook Social Connector

Difficulty: ○○○○

PROBLEM You have just met a new potential business partner. After entering his contact information you now want to connect with him on LinkedIn.

SOLUTION Use the **Outlook Social Connector**. Introduced in Outlook 2010, the new **Outlook Social Connector** links Outlook with popular social media networks. With the Social Connector, you can send and receive contact requests and view your contact's activity, such as status updates, comments, and alerts, without leaving your desktop.

Step-by-Step

Install Social Network Provider Add-In

For each external social network you wish to connect to, you will need to install that provider's Outlook add-in. These are not provided by Microsoft. Our example will use **LinkedIn's** add-in.

1. To find add-ins for other networks such as Facebook, Viadeo, and Xing, for example, click the **View** tab, then click the **People Pane** dropdown button  in the **People Pane** group.

2. Select **Account Settings** B from the dropdown menu to open the setup dialog box.

3. Click the **View social network providers available online** link C to open Micorosoft Office.com's **Outlook Social Connector Partner Listing** page in your web browser.

4. Click on the social network you want to install , then follow the directions for that provider.

If your organization uses Microsoft Office SharePoint Server 2010, the Social Connector can automatically connect with local SharePoint sites and display local coworker's activity items.

Open the People Pane

To access the **Social Connector** features, you will need to be able to see Outlook 2010's new **People Pane**. To expand the **People Pane**, click on the **View** tab, then click the **People Pane** dropdown button. Select **Normal** from the dropdown menu to open the pane below the reading pane.

CONTINUE

19 Outlook Social Connector (continued)

Step-by-Step

Connect Outlook to a Social Network

1. Click the **View** tab, then click the **People Pane** dropdown button  A in the **People Pane** group.

2. Select **Account Settings** B from the dropdown menu to open the setup dialog box.

3. Click **Next** if you receive the introduction pane.

4. Under **Social Network Accounts**, select the social network you want to connect to C.

5. Type in your account information and password for that social network D, then click the **Connect** button.

6. The dialog box will update to reflect the account you are connected to E.

7. Connect to another network, or click **Finish** to close the dialog box.

8. If a person in your contact list matches a contact on the social network you have connected to, their activity on those networks will be available in the **People Pane** from an email or contact window. Click the **Activities** tab F to view items your contact has shared or interacted with. Click the **Status Updates** G tab to see recent status posts.

Step-by-Step

Invite a Contact to Your Social Network from Outlook

1. Open a contact window for the person you want to invite.

2. In the **People Pane**, click the **Add** button .

3. Select the social network you want to connect through .

4. Click **Continue** to answer the question **Are you sure you want to add this person on LinkedIn?** A connection request will be sent through the social network (in this example, LinkedIn) to your contact. While Outlook is waiting for a reply, a **pending icon** will be added to their profile on your **people pane**.

Caution: Be aware that when you send a connection request, your contact will receive an email from the network (LinkedIn, Facebook, etc.) Be sure only to send requests to contacts who will not mind networking with you in this way.

20 | Microsoft Outlook Tasks View

The following section will help you create and manage your To-Do lists. With Outlook Tasks, you can keep your own projects organized, track due dates so you won't miss deadlines, and assign tasks to other members of your organization.

The following tips will all refer to the Tasks View unless otherwise noted. To make sure your Outlook window is in the Tasks View, check to see if the Tasks View button **A** is selected at the bottom of the Navigation Pane.

If you do not see the Navigation Pane on the left side of your Outlook window, you may need to open it. Click the Navigation Pane button **B** in the Layout group on the View tab and then select Normal or Minimized **C** from the dropdown menu.

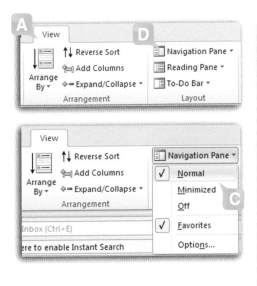

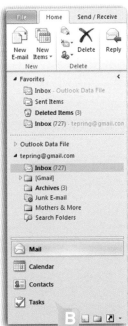

20 | Create a New Task

Difficulty: ○○○○

PROBLEM You want to write a to-do list of all the tasks necessary to complete the new project you've just been assigned. You would like a way to organize your tasks by project and keep track of due dates for milestones.

SOLUTION Create a **New Task** in the **To-Do** bar. In addition to creating your list of necessary tasks, you can keep it organized by setting start and due dates, flagging completed tasks, and deferring tasks that have yet to be completed.

Option 1 – You may be doing many different things when you realize you need to create a new task for your to-do list such as responding to an email, managing your calendar, speaking on the phone, etc. Outlook gives you many ways to create a new task so that you can do so without interrupting the task you are currently working on.

Option 1 – Create a Task from the Task View

 **Step-by-Step**

1. On the **Home** tab, in the **New** group, click the **New Task** button  to open a **New Task** window.

2. Type in a name or description of the task in the **Subject:** text box **B**. You can also type more detail about the task in the **Task Body Pane** **C**.

3. Set the date for when the task needs to be completed in the **Due date:** box **D**. You can also set a **Start date:** in the **Start date:** box **E**. 💡 ⚡

4. If you would like Outlook to send you a reminder when the due date is approaching, click the **Reminder** checkbox **F** and set the date and time for when you would like to receive the notice.

5. In the **Tags** group, you can mark a task as **High Importance** or **Low Importance** 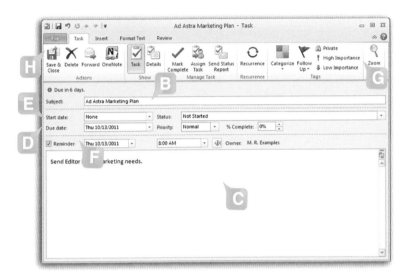 to help you prioritize when you are working from your Tasks list.

6. Click **Save & Close** to save the task and add it to your **To-Do** list.

Option 2 – Create a Task from the To-Do Bar

Use this option to quickly add a task from any view. Your **To-Do** bar is located in the bottom right corner of your Outlook desktop and appears in all views by default, unless you have customized your view.

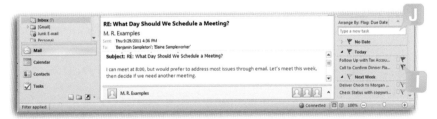

1. Double click inside the **Type a new task** text box in the **To-Do bar** to open a **New Task** window.

2. Fill out the task details as described in Option 1, then click **Save & Close**.

OR

1. Type in a name or description of the task in the **Type a new task** text box in the **To-Do bar** 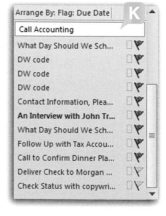.

2. Hit the **ENTER** key. This will add the task to your **To-Do** list with today's date.

 Quickest Click: For a quick way to add the **Follow Up** flag to an Outlook item so that it will show up in your To-Do list, drag and drop items into the **To-Do bar** or onto the **Tasks** tab in the navigation pane.

1. Click on the item you wish to copy into a task, then drag the item to the To-Do bar. Note: You can be in any view to use this method. The item can be an email message (as in this example), a calendar item, contact card, or note.

2. The cursor will change to indicate that you are dragging an item. Place your cursor in the To-Do bar at the place where you want your task assigned. A red line will indicate where your task will go when you release the item. Or, drag your item over the **Tasks** tab on the **Navigation Pane**.

Adding a task in this way copies the item in your **To-Do** list with a **Follow Up flag**, but does not assign Start or Due dates.

Quickest Click: Use the **Follow Up** dropdown menu to quickly set due dates without having to look up dates in the calendar. Choose from the options to assign a task a due date of **Today, Tomorrow, This week** (assigns a due date of Friday of the current week), **Next week** (assigns a due date of Friday of the following week.)

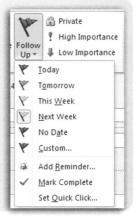

Bright Idea: For tasks that you repeat on a regular schedule, such as a report you must mail every Monday to your department, you can set up a recurring task. Click the **Recurrence** button in the **Recurrence** group on the **Task** tab in your task window to open the **Task Recurrence** dialog box. *See Also: Set a Recurring Appointment.*

Specify how you want the task to recur, then click **OK** to close the dialog box and save your recurrence settings.

21 | Mark a Task as Complete

Difficulty: ○○○○

PROBLEM You just completed the expense report that was on your task list as due for today. You want to remove it from your To-Do list and let your boss, who assigned you the task, know that you have finished it.

SOLUTION Mark the task as Complete. **The Mark Complete** option puts a strike through the task in your task list to show that it has been accomplished. The person who assigned the task can clearly and easily see that your assigned task has been completed. If they also requested a status report when they assigned the task to you, Outlook will automatically send an update informing them that you have finished.

See Also: Change the Task View

Step-by-Step

1. Click on the **Tasks** folder **A** in your navigation pane, then select the task you wish to mark as complete **B**.

2. Click the **Mark Complete** button **C** in the **Manage Task** group on the **Home** tab. Outlook will cross out the task, and put a checkmark in the flag column to indicate the task has been completed. ✹

Quickest Click: Right-click any task in the task pane or To-Do bar, then select **Mark Complete** from the fly-out menu.

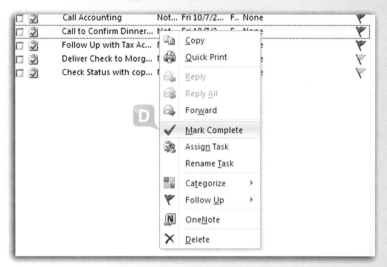

22 Assign a Task to Another Outlook User

Difficulty: ○○○○

PROBLEM You are the lead on an important project, and you must assign an important task to one of your team members.

SOLUTION Use the **Assign Task** option to email a task or list of tasks to another person. By assigning tasks, you can manage which of your team members is in charge of what task, and follow up with them as needed. You can also watch their progress as they work on the task and receive a notice when the task is complete.

See Also: Create A New Task; Accept or Decline a Task Assignment

Step-by-Step

1. Open a New Task window and fill out the task details, or open an existing task.

2. Click the **Assign Task** button  in the **Manage Task** group on the **Task** tab.

3. Outlook will open an email task message window. In the **To...** text box  fill in the address of the person who will be responsible for the task. ⚠

4. If you want to receive notice when the task is marked as complete, check the **Send me a status report when this task is complete** checkbox.

5. To track the progress of a task as it is being worked on, click the **Keep an updated copy of this task on my task list** checkbox. This will allow you to view the status of a task as it is changed by the task owner.

6. Click **Send**. The task will be sent to the recipient to be accepted or declined. If the recipient accepts the task, they become the owner of that task and the only person who can make changes to the task. When they make changes to the task, all copies of the task will be updated.

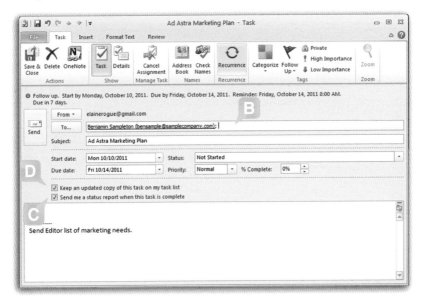

Caution: You cannot keep an updated copy of a task if you assign it to more than one person at a time. If you have more than one person working on a project, it is best to break the work into smaller individual tasks that you can track and for which you can maintain accountability.

23 | Accept or Decline a Task Assignment

Difficulty: ⭕⭕⭕⭕

PROBLEM You have just been assigned a task from your project manager, and you need to let him know that you accept the task.

SOLUTION Accept the task. Accepting a task confirms with the person who assigned the task that you will be responsible for the contents of that task. When you accept a task, Outlook designates you the permanent owner of that task, and you will be the only person who can change or update the task. If your manager maintains a copy of the task, he or she will be able view the changes you make as you work on it.

Step-by-Step

1. When someone sends you a task assignment, you will receive an email message with the task details they have specified. To accept the task, click the **Accept** button **A** in the **Respond** group on the message window's **Task** tab. ⚠

2. To decline the task, click the **Decline** button **B**.

3. Choose **Edit the response before sending** radio button to add a message to the reply notice, or click the **Send the response now** button to send the notice without making changes.

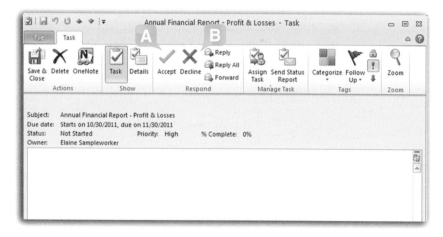

Caution: When you accept a task, you become the permanent owner of that task and are now the only person who can update and edit it. If you cannot complete the task or need someone else to track the status of the task, you must re-assign the task to them.

24 Change the Task View

Difficulty: ○○○○

PROBLEM You have been offered the chance to represent your company at a trade show, so you need to make sure you have all your tasks either completed or reassigned before you leave for several days. You want to view all of your tasks that are due in the next seven days.

SOLUTION Change your task appearance settings. Outlook gives you many tools to organize and view your tasks so you can find the items you are looking for and plan your work efficiently. By changing your appearance settings, you can sort your tasks in a number of ways, such as by date, category, or priority. You can customize how tasks appear, including the order of the tasks and the number of tasks shown.

Step-by-Step

1. Click the **View** tab, then click the **Change View** dropdown button  in the **Current View** group.

2. Click an option in the dropdown menu. Outlook has provided several common views to choose from:

   - **Detailed** – Multi-column view with twelve of the most common columns included.
   - **Simple List** – Multi-column view with only six of the most common columns included.
   - **To-Do List** – Displays your tasks in the To-Do format.
   - **Prioritized** – Displays tasks by priority setting in the Simple List format.
   - **Active** – Displays only the active tasks. Completed tasks will not be shown.
   - **Completed** – Displays only completed tasks.

- **Today** – Displays only those tasks that are due today.
- **Next 7 Days** – Displays only those tasks that are due in the next seven days. In our **Problem** example, this is the view you would choose B.
- **Overdue** – Displays only overdue tasks.
- **Assigned** – Displays tasks assigned to other owners.
- **Server Tasks** – Displays tasks that have been synchronized with a SharePoint task list.

3. To further sort your tasks within a particular view, choose from more options in the **Arrangements** selection box:

- **Categories** – Sort your tasks by category.
- **Start Date & Due Date** – Sort your tasks by Start Date or Due Date.
- **Type** – Sort by type of task.
- **Importance** – Sort your tasks by priority setting C.
- **Assignment** – Sort tasks by who has been assigned the task.
- **Modified Date** – Sort tasks by the date they were last modified.

Click the **Show in Groups** toggle D to group your tasks visually by the criteria you have specified.

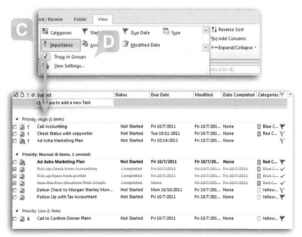

This example shows a **Detailed View**, sorted by **Importance**, with the **Show in Groups** toggle on.

Quickest Click: In a multi-column view, such as the **Detailed View**, you can easily sort by column simply by clicking on the column's heading 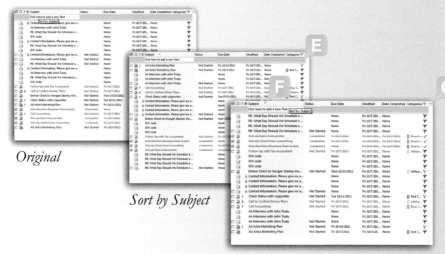 **E**. Click a second time to reverse the sort **F**. A sort arrow will appear in the column, indicating the sort direction **G**.

Original

Sort by Subject

Sort by Subject Reversed

Hot Tip: You can customize your views even further from the **Advanced View Settings** dialog box. Select the view that is closest to what you are looking for, then click the **View Settings** button **H**. In the dialog box, you can pick which columns you want and the order they appear **I**. You can filter items and specify multiple sort orders (Sort by Date Due, then Priority, then Subject, for example.) Once you have created the view you need, click **OK** to apply the settings.

Bright Idea: If you find that you regularly modify one of Outlook's preset views to see your items in the order you want them, you can save your settings as a custom view. On the **View** tab, in the **Current View** group, click the **Change View** dropdown button and then select **Save Current View As a New View** . Type a name for your view in the dialog box, select which folders you want the view to apply to, then click **OK**. Your new view will appear in the **Change View** dropdown menu for future use.

25 Print Your Tasks

Difficulty: ○○○○

PROBLEM You are going to be out of the office for the day and want to print a list of all the tasks that are due this week.

SOLUTION Microsoft Outlook allows you to print one task, or a list of tasks, from a number of different views. After printing your tasks, you can easily distribute the printout to members of your team or take it with you to be used at a different location.

In Outlook 2010, all print functionality has been moved under the **File** tab into the **Backstage View.** The Print procedure is the same for Mail, Calendar, Tasks, and Notes, giving you one place to specify your print settings and preview your printouts.

See Also: Change the Task View

Step-by-Step

1. Use the **View** tab to sort and filter your task list until the set of tasks you want to print are displayed the way you want them.

2. Click on the **File** tab A, then click the **Print** option B. Print Options and Settings will appear next to the **Print Preview** pane C.

3. Under the **Settings** heading, choose from the Style options available to you D. The preview pane will update to display the setting you have chosen.

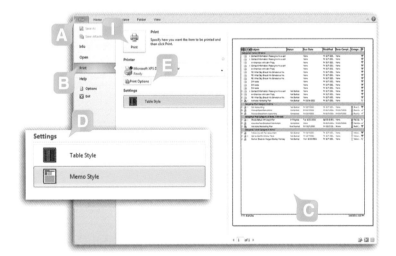

4. Click the **Print Options** button 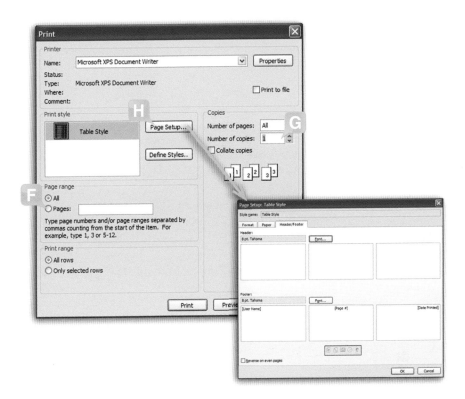 to open the **Print** dialog box. From the **Print** dialog box, you can choose to print specific pages or a page range , print multiple copies , and create Headers or Footers for your printouts using the **Page Setup** dialog box .

5. Click **Print** to send your document to the printer or **Preview** to return to the **Backstage View**.

6. When you are ready to print from the **Backstage View**, click the **Print** button .

26 | Send a Status Report

Difficulty: ◯◯◯◯

PROBLEM Your boss has asked you to update her on the status of the report that you have been assigned to complete.

SOLUTION Send a **Status Report**. Outlook gives you an easy way to send status updates on tasks that you own or manage. When you use the **Send Status Report** feature, Outlook automatically includes the original task subject and details, plus the current **% Complete** setting in an email message that you can forward to anyone who needs the information. As a task owner, this gives you an easy way to keep your boss informed. As a manager, you can request and receive updates on all the tasks you are tracking in a standardized format.

Step-by-Step

1. Open the task in a task window and make sure the task is up-to-date. Click on the **Status** dropdown menu **A** to select the current status setting. Click the up or down arrows to specify a **% Complete** setting **B**.

2. For more reporting fields, click the **Details** button **C** in the **Show** group. In this pane, you can update status such as **Total work hours, Actual work hours, Mileage**, and **Billing information.**

3. Click the **Send Status Report** button **D** in the **Manage Task** group on the **Task** tab.

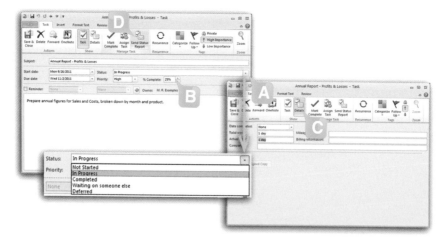

4. An email message window will open with the task's status information included in the body of the message 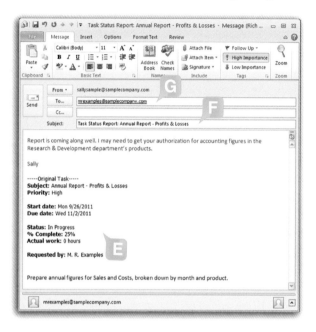, and the name of the task in the **Subject** line . Enter an email address for the recipient in the **To…** line .

5. Add any additional information needed in the message body, then click **Send**.

27 | Set the Task Default Options

Difficulty: ○○○○

PROBLEM You want to change the color of overdue and completed tasks, and you want to make sure you are reminded when you have tasks due today.

SOLUTION Change the appearance of your tasks. Outlook gives you several ways to customize how your tasks appear. You can modify the fonts used or categorize the tasks into an easier-to-manage format. By changing the appearance of your tasks, you can make it easier to keep track of the items that you have been assigned and when the items are due.

Step-by-Step

1. Click the **File** tab **A**, then click the **Options** button **B** to open the **Outlook Options** dialog box.

2. Click on the **Tasks** tab **C** to view setting options for your tasks and to-do items:
    *   Reminders – Automatically set reminders when a due date is specified by clicking the **Set reminders on tasks with due dates** checkbox **D**. To choose what time of day the reminder will be delivered, make a selection from the **Default reminder time:** dropdown menu.
    *   Status reports – Choose defaults for saving copies of tasks that you assign to other people, and choose whether you want to receive a notice when assignments are marked complete.
    *   Tasks Colors – To change the default color of an overdue task, click the dropdown arrow next to **Overdue task color:** **E**. Choose the color you want for overdue tasks from the dropdown menu. Choose a default color for tasks that have been marked complete from the **Completed task color:** dropdown menu **F**.

3. Click **OK** to apply the new default settings.

Hot Tip: The **View Settings** dialog box lets you customize not only how tasks should look, such as font and color, but also what conditions should be met to display them a certain way. Changes made to one view in this way will apply only to that view. For example, if you make overdue tasks blue instead of red in the **Detailed** view, they will still appear as red in the **Simple List** or **Active** view. *See Also: Change the Task View* to combine these steps with the steps for saving a modified view to create truly customized organization.

1. Click on the **View Settings** button in the **View** group on the **View** tab to open the **Advanced View Settings** dialog box.

2. Click the **Conditional Formatting...** button to open the **Conditional Formatting** dialog box.

3. Select the **Rule** that you want to change.

4. To change text appearance for a task that meets the rule's condition, click the **Font...** button, then make your formatting choices from the **Font** dialog box. Customize font, color, size, and any effects you want for your rule, then click **OK**.

5. To add a new rule to the view's conditional formatting options:

   • Click the **Add** button.

   • Type a name for your new Rule in the **Name:** text box, then click the **Condition...** button to open the **Filter** dialog box. Specify the conditions for the rule, then click **OK**.

   • To change text appearance for the tasks that meet the new rule's condition, click the **Font...** button and follow directions above.

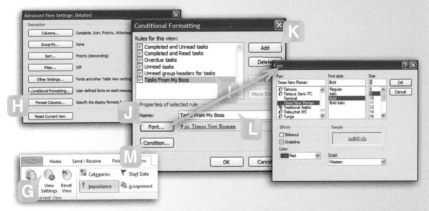

6. Click **OK** to close the **Conditional Formatting** dialog box and apply the settings, then click **OK** to close the **Advanced View Settings** dialog box and save your settings for that view only.

28 | Create a New Note

Difficulty: ○○○○

PROBLEM You want to keep a reminder of your sales goals on your desktop where you can reference quickly without opening a text editor or switching to Outlook Views.

SOLUTION Create a Note. Instead of writing notes on scraps of paper that can easily be misplaced, create a Note to leave open on your desktop. You can have as many notes open as you wish. Notes are useful for information that you reference frequently, for quickly jotting something down that you want to file more carefully later, or for text that you might need to copy between several documents or multiple programs.

Step-by-Step

1. Create a note from any Outlook view by clicking the **Notes** button **A** in the bottom left corner of your Outlook window. This will open the **Notes** view.

2. Click the **New Note** button **B** in the **New** group on the **Home** tab. A blank note will appear on your desktop **C**. Any existing notes you have created will appear in the reading pane **D**.

3. Type your text into the body of the note. You can resize the note by grabbing and dragging the corner size handle  so that your note shows all the text you have typed. Drag the note any location on your screen where you will be able to easily see it. Leave the note to open while you work for quick access to the text.

4. Text is automatically saved when you type in a note window. When you are done viewing your note, click the **Close** button.

5. To open or edit an existing note, click the **Notes** button A from anywhere in Outlook and then double-click on the note in the **Notes View** reading pane D.

29 Change the Color of a Note

Difficulty: ○○○○

PROBLEM You use the Notes feature to jot down customer comments when you are working with them over the phone. Later, you use those notes to create tasks and to-do lists and write follow up email messages. But since you work on several projects at once, you usually have several notes at a time that need to be addressed. You would like a way to quickly identify which reminder note goes with which project.

SOLUTION Change the color of your notes to organize them by project using the Categorize function. You can arrange your notes by color to easily track which notes belong to which project.

See Also: Categorize Items

Step-by-Step

1. To add a category color to an open note, click the note icon in the top left corner **A** to open the dropdown menu.

2. Click the **Categorize** option **B**, then choose from the list of categories available.

3. To add a color to a closed note, click the **Notes** button **C** in the bottom left corner of your Outlook window, then click once on the note you want to categorize in the reading pane **D**. ⚡

4. Click the **Categorize** button in the **Tags** group on the **Home** tab .

5. Select a category  from the dropdown menu for your note to apply that color .

 Quickest Click: Add a category to a closed note from the reading pane by right-clicking on the note, then selecting **Categorize** from the fly-out menu . Select the category you want to apply the color to the note.

30 | Track Your Time in the Journal

Difficulty: ◯◯◯◯

PROBLEM As an independent marketing consultant, you bill by the hour and want to track the time you work on each project. Since your billable time is valuable, you also want to increase your productivity. It would be very helpful to have a way to see where your time goes throughout the day so you can identify time-wasting activities.

SOLUTION Enable the Journal function to keep track of how you are using your time. Outlook Journal keeps a recording of any interaction that you tell it to track, including time writing email messages, assigning tasks, and scheduling meetings. The Journal can also create a timeline of files and documents you have worked on in other Office programs such as Word or Excel. This feature allows you to see where your time is being used productively and where your time could be used more effectively.

See Also: Change the Task View

Step-by-Step

Turn on Journal Tracking

1. Click the **File** tab A , then click the **Options** button B to open the **Outlook Options** dialog box.

2. Click the **Notes and Journal** tab C to view journal options, then click the **Journal Options…** button D to open the **Journal Options** dialog box.

3. Check the actions you want automatically recorded:

- **Automatically record these items:** Check the activities you want recorded .

- **For these contacts:** Check the contacts for whom you want activities recorded. Check your current clients to record the time you spend communicating with them, for example **F**.

- **Also record files from:** Tell the Journal what other programs you use that you want included in your journal **G**.

4. Click **OK** when your settings are complete, then click **OK** to close the **Outlook Options** dialog box and save your changes.

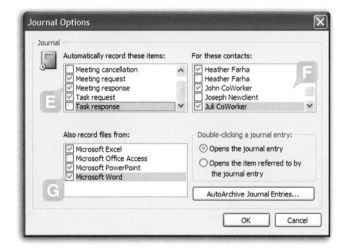

Step-by-Step

View Your Journal Entries

1. Click the **Folder** icon  **H** at the bottom of your **Navigation Pane**, and then select the **Journal** folder **I** to open the **Journal View**.

2. All work that has been recorded will appear in the reading pane of the **Journal View** **J**. In the default **Timeline** view, journal entries are organized by **Entry Type.** To find when you last updated your Excel spreadsheet of customer addresses, look under the **Entry Type: Microsoft Excel** heading **K**.

3. You can change the way your entries are sorted and arranged from the **Current View** selection box **L**, or from the **View** tab.

Bright Idea: Add the **Journal** button to your **Navigation Pane** for quick access to your **Journal Timeline**. Click on the **Configure Buttons** arrow M at the bottom of the navigation pane. Select **Add or Remove Buttons** N, then click the **Journal** button O to add it to the bottom of the pane.

Click the **Journal** button P to open the Journal View.

31 | Manually Create a Journal Entry

Difficulty: ◐◐◐◐

PROBLEM You are dialing a new client and want to track the time you spend with him on the phone.

SOLUTION While some activities may be automatically added to the Journal, other activities, such as time spent on the phone with a new client or an in-person meeting, need to be manually added. You can use the journal to keep track of how much time is spent with a client, how much they should be billed, and any other items that you wish to remember.

Step-by-Step

1. From any view within Outlook, click the **New Items** button  in the **New** group on the **Home** tab.

2. Choose the **More Items** option B from the dropdown menu, then click **Journal Entry** C to open a blank **Journal Entry.**

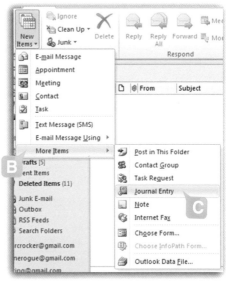

3. Fill out your Journal entry with the information you want to record:

   - Type an entry topic in the **Subject:** textbox .
   - Type a description of how your time was spent in the entry body, and select an **Entry type:** from the dropdown menu E.
   - Enter your **Start time:** F and **Duration**: time G.

4. When your edits are complete, click **Save & Close** to log the entry in your Journal.

The following section will help you create and manage your appointments. With Outlook Calendar, you can keep your own calendar organized, set reminders so you won't miss meetings, and invite other members of your organization to events you are scheduling. If you are using Microsoft Exchange Server, you can also view your colleague's calendars to make scheduling much easier.

The following tips will all refer to the Calendar View unless otherwise noted. To make sure your Outlook window is in the Calendar View, check to see if the Calendar View button A is selected at the bottom of the Navigation Pane.

If you do not see the Navigation Pane on the left side of your Outlook window, you may need to open it. Click the Navigation Pane button B in the Layout group on the View tab, then select Normal or Minimized C from the dropdown menu.

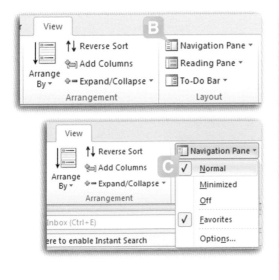

32 | Create an Appointment

Difficulty: ⭕⭕⭕⭕

PROBLEM You just set a lunch appointment with a new potential client that you want to make sure you don't forget it.

SOLUTION Create an appointment in your Outlook calendar. Recording an appointment in your calendar will not only help you remember the event but also help you organize and categorize your time. By keeping your calendar up to date, you can avoid embarrassing conflicts.

See Also: Change the Task View

Step-by-Step

Create an Appointment

1. Click the **New Appointment** button A in the **New** group on the **Home** tab to open a **New Appointment** window.

2. Type a meeting description in the **Subject:** textbox B.

3. Enter the location of the meeting in the **Location:** textbox C.

4. Select a **Start time:** and **End:** time for your meeting in the dropdown menus D.

5. Type additional details in the appointment body E.

6. Click **Save & Close** to save your appointment to your calendar.

Your appointment will appear in the reading pane of the **Calendar View** F.
To change the view so that you are looking at only a single day G or the whole
month H, choose from view options in the **Arrange** group on the **Home** tab.

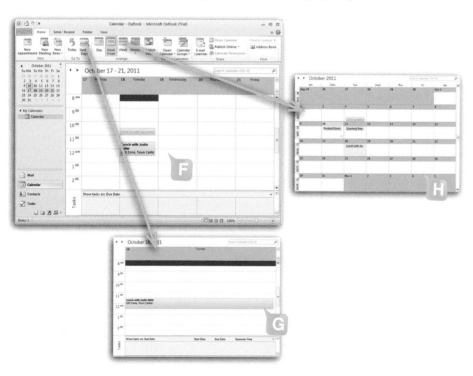

33 | Set a Recurring Appointment

Difficulty: ○○○○

PROBLEM You have a regular department meeting every Monday morning at 9:00 a.m. You would like a way to tell Outlook to automatically put the meeting in your calendar every week instead of having to enter it by hand over and over.

SOLUTION Set a Recurring Appointment. You only need to create your department meeting once and then indicate that you would like that particular appointment to repeat on all Monday mornings. With the Recurrence setting, you can specify how often an appointment will repeat (daily, weekly, monthly, etc.) and how long or how many times the appointment should repeat.

See Also: Create an Appointment

Step-by-Step

1. Open a New Appointment window and fill in the date, time, and details for the appointment series.

2. Before you save the appointment, click the **Recurrence** button **A** in the **Options** group on the **Appointment** tab in the appointment window to open the **Appointment Recurrence** dialog box.

3. Confirm the time for the series under the **Appointment time** heading **B**.

4. Click a radio button under the **Recurrence pattern** heading to choose an interval between meetings. Each radio button will open related pattern options:

- **Daily** – Choose between every day of the week or weekdays only.

- **Weekly** – Choose which day of the week the meeting will repeat. Enter a number in the **Recur every ___ week(s) on:** text box C if your meeting will skip weeks. Enter "2" if you meet every other week, for example.

- **Monthly** – Choose the day of the month that the meeting will repeat by date D or by day of the week within a specific week E. Enter a number in the **every ___ month(s)** text box if your meeting will skip months. Enter a "3" if you meet quarterly, for example.

- **Yearly** – Choose the day of the year that the meeting will repeat by date F or by day of the week within a specific week and month G. Enter a number in the **Recur every ___ years(s)** text box if your meeting will skip months. Enter a "2" if you meet every other year, for example.

CONTINUE

5. If you want the series to end rather than repeat indefinitely, set an end date by number of occurrences  or by date .

6. Click **OK** when you are finished defining your recurrence preferences.

7. Click **Save & Close** to save your appointment to your calendar. You will see the appointment repeated on the days you specified in the reading pane.

Caution: When modifying an appointment that is recurring, remember that the changes can affect every instance of the meeting. When you open an appointment that is recurring, Outlook will give you the **Open Recurring Item** dialog box.

Click **Open this occurrence** to change *only* the specific appointment you clicked on. Use this when a meeting is cancelled or changed one time, but will return to its regular schedule the next time.

Click **Open to series** to change every recurrence of the appointment. Use this when every instance of the meeting needs to be updated.

34 Schedule a Meeting

Difficulty: ○○○○

PROBLEM You are working on a project with two other colleagues. You want to schedule a meeting for all three of you to discuss your progress and plan your next steps.

SOLUTION Create a New Meeting. This feature allows you to send a request to your co-workers to meet you in a specific place at a specific time, and your co-workers can have their response sent directly to your inbox.

See Also: Create a New Email Message

Step-by-Step

Invite Attendees to a Meeting

1. Click the **New Meeting** button  in the **New** group on the **Home** tab to open a meeting request window.

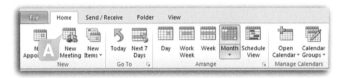

2. Type a meeting description in the **Subject:** textbox **B**.

3. Enter the location of the meeting in the **Location:** textbox **C**.

4. Select a **Start time:** and **End time:** for your meeting in the dropdown menus **D**.

5. Type additional details in the appointment body **E**.

6. Enter the email addresses for the other attendees in the **To...** line **F**. You can type the addresses, select from your address book by clicking the **To...** button, or type the first letters of the recipient's name, and then choose an auto-complete option.

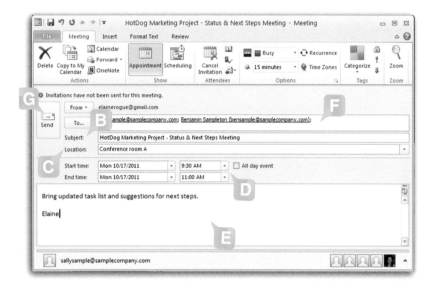

7. When your meeting description is complete, click the **Send** button G. Your recipients will receive the meeting request in their inbox, and the appointment will appear on your calendar.

8. When an attendee responds to your request, you will receive an email message in your inbox with their reply.

CONTINUE

Step-by-Step

Respond to a Meeting Request

1. When someone sends you a meeting request, you will receive an email message with the meeting details they have specified:

    *   To accept the invitation, click the **Accept** button 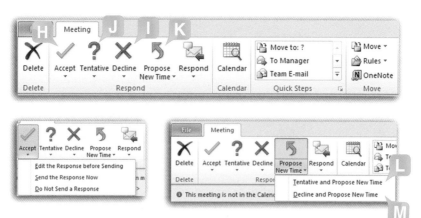 in the **Respond** group on the message window's **Meeting** tab.
    *   To decline the invitation, click the **Decline** button .
    *   If you are not certain about your availability, but wish the organizer to know you have received the invitation, click the **Tentative** response button .

    Each of the above will open a dropdown menu. Choose **Send the Response Now** to send the meeting planner your reply, or choose **Edit the Response before Sending** to add a message in the invitation reply. Choose **Do Not Send a Response** if you do not want any reply sent.

2. To propose an alternative meeting time, click the **Propose New Time** button . Choose whether you are:

    *   Tentatively accepting the meeting and making a time change proposal , or
    *   Declining the meeting and suggesting a new time that you can attend .

        When you make your selection, the **Propose New Time** dialog box will open.

3. Set a new **Meeting start** and **Meeting end** time in the dropdown menus , then click **Propose Time** .

4. Type any comments you want in the body of the **New Time Proposed** meeting response message , then click **Send**. A message with the proposed time will be sent to the meeting organizer.

Although you can propose a new time, the meeting organizer must accept the new time for the meeting to be changed in the calendar. The meeting organizer can also choose not to allow attendees to make new time proposals. If the organizer has restricted meeting proposals, the **Propose New Time** button will not be available.

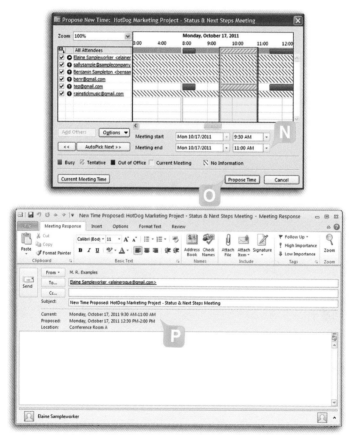

35 | Create a New Calendar

Difficulty: ○○○○

PROBLEM You manage the use of the conference room. Right now, you are entering the room's activity in your own color coded and categorized calendar. It is difficult to see when the room is available because it is mixed together with all of your appointments. When appointments overlap, it is even more confusing. You want to find an easier way to keep track of when the conference room is in use.

SOLUTION Create a New Calendar. Creating a unique calendar for the conference room scheduling will help keep you organized by separating your conference room appointments from all of your other appointments. You can create as many calendars as you wish. For example, you could create one calendar to keep track of items for your home office and another to track sales calls outside of the office.

Step-by-Step

Create a New Calendar

1. Click the **Folder** tab, then click the **New Calendar** button  in the **New** group to open the **Create New Folder** dialog box.

2. Type a name for the calendar in the **Name:** text box **B**.

3. Make sure the **Calendar** folder is selected in the **Select where to place the folder:** pane **C**.

4. Click **OK** to create the calendar. The new calendar folder will appear in your **Navigation Pane**, under the **Calendar** folder **D**.

Step-by-Step

View Multiple Calendars

If you have created multiple calendars, you can view some, all, or only one at a time. You can choose to view the calendars side by side or mingled together in an overlay view.

1. Check the check box beside the calendar(s) you want to view . If you choose multiple calendars, the default setting is a side by side view. Your calendars will appear next to each other in the reading pane **F**. Uncheck a calendar or click the **Close** button on the Calendar's tab **G** to remove it from your view.

2. To overlay your calendars and view appointments merged into a single pane, click the **View in Overlay Mode** button **H** on the **Calendar** tab. Click the **Overlay Mode** button again to return to side-by-side view.

Difficulty: ○○○○

PROBLEM Your workday starts at 9:00 a.m. and ends at 6:00 p.m., and you want the calendar to accurately represent your workday.

SOLUTION Changing your Calendar options will allow you to alter your start/end time, set what days you're in the office, and even change how early you want your calendar to remind you before you have to get to your meeting.

Step-by-Step

1. Click the **File** tab **A**, then click the **Options** button **B** to open the **Outlook Options** dialog box.

2. Click on the **Calendar** tab **C** to view setting options for your tasks and to-do items:

   • **Work time** – Under this heading, you can set your default work hours by changing the **Start time:** and **End time: D** settings, specify which days of the week you work **E**, and customize what day you want your calendar week to start on **F**.

   • **Calendar options** – Set the default for how long before a meeting a reminder will be given **G**. You can also enable alternate calendars and add holiday date information under this heading.

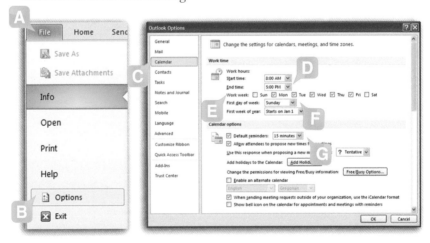

- **Display options** – Customize calendar colors and fonts; specify layout and view preferences.

- **Time zones** – Change the time zone your calendar is set to, or add a second time zone for multi-location scheduling.

- **Scheduling assistant** – Specify which details are shown in **ScreenTip** and the scheduling grid.
- **Resource scheduling** – Set options for replies and access to calendars for non-human resources, such as a conference room or other meeting venue.

3. Click **OK** when you have completed your changes to apply the new default settings.

37 | Print a Calendar

Difficulty: ⭕⭕⭕⭕

PROBLEM You are often on the road without computer access, so you would like to print your calendar on a weekly basis.

SOLUTION Printing your calendar is a convenient way to keep yourself on track without having to access your computer. Microsoft Outlook allows you to print everything from specific calendar items to a whole calendar, depending on your needs.

Step-by-Step

1. Click on the **File** tab **A**, then click the **Print** option **B**. **Print Options** and **Settings** will appear next to the **Print Preview** pane **C**.

2. Choose the style of printout you want from the list under the **Settings** heading **D**. The **Preview Pane** will update to display the style you have chosen.

3. Click the **Print Options** button to open the **Print** dialog box. From the **Print** dialog box, you can choose to print specific pages or a page range, you can print multiple copies, and create Headers or Footers for your printouts in the **Page Setup** dialog box.

4. To select a specific date range to print, set the **Start** and **End** dates in the **Print range** section.

5. Click **Print** to send your document to the printer, or **Preview** to return to the **Backstage View**.

6. When you are ready to print from the **Backstage View**, click the **Print** button.

38 | Create a Calendar Group

Difficulty: ⭕⭕⭕⭕

PROBLEM You manage the calendars for all the conference rooms and for two different executives. You would like an easy way to view just the conference rooms, without having to click several calendars off and on each time you need to help someone schedule a room.

SOLUTION Create a Calendar Group. A Calendar Group lets you organize multiple calendars into easy-to-access groups based upon your own categorization. Calendar groups can include SharePoint or other external internet calendars and resource calendars, such as conference rooms, in addition to colleague calendars and your own personal calendars.

Option – Outlook gives you two ways to create calendar groups. Choose the method that best fits your needs.

Option 1 – Create a Calendar Group from your View

Use this method when you have already created calendars for the resources or topics you are tracking.

Step-by-Step

1. In the **Calendar View**, select the set of calendars you usually view together by clicking their checkboxes in the **Navigation Pane** A.

2. Click the **Calendar Groups** button  in the **Manage Calendars** group on the
    Home tab.

3. Select **Save as New Calendar Group** C from the dropdown menu to open the
    Create New Calendar Group dialog box.

4. Type a name for your Calendar Group in the text box D, then click **OK**.

5. The calendars that you have grouped will appear nested under the group name
    E in the **Navigation Pane**.

6. Check and uncheck the box next to the group's name to view or hide the entire
    group.

7. To add a new calendar to a group that has already been created, simply click on
    the new calendar in the **Navigation Pane**, then drag and drop it on top of the
    group name F.

Option 2 – Create a Calendar Group from Contacts

Use this method when you want to group calendars of co-workers or people from your contacts list.

Step-by-Step

1. Click the **Calendar Groups** button **B** in the **Manage Calendars** group on the **Home** tab.

2. Select **Save as New Calendar Group** **G** from the dropdown menu to open the **Create New Calendar Group** dialog box.

3. Type a name for your **Calendar Group** in the text box **H**, then click **OK** to open the **Select Name: Contacts** dialog box.

4. Select a contact whose calendar you want to view from the contacts pane **I**, then click **Group Members > button** **J** to add them to the group list. Repeat until all the contacts you want to view in a group have been added.

5. Click **OK**.

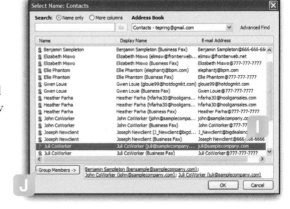

6. The calendars that you have grouped will appear nested under the group name **K** in the **Navigation Pane**.

7. Check and uncheck the box next to the group's name to view or hide the entire group.

8. To add a new contact's calendar to your group, click the **Schedule View** button **L** in the **Arrange** group.

9. Type the name of the contact in the **Add a Calendar** textbox **M** in the reading pane under the list of calendars.

10. Select the correct name **N** from the **Check Names** dialog box, then click **OK** to add the new contact to your calendar group.

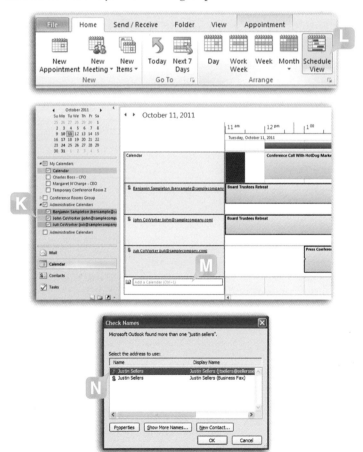

39 | Share a Calendar

Difficulty: ○○○○

PROBLEM Your boss now wants you to set all his appointments. You need a way to access his calendar and permission to make changes to it.

SOLUTION Share a calendar with another Microsoft Exchange Server user.

Outlook gives users several ways to share calendar information. Sharing by email sends an attachment snapshot of a calendar to the recipient's inbox. This method can give your recipient an idea about your schedule and what time you may have available in the coming days, but it will not stay up-to-date or allow the recipient to respond to or edit the calendar.

Outlook also supports internet calendar sharing. This option is useful for sharing calendar information with people who do not have access to Microsoft Exchange Server. When you publish a calendar to Office.com, you can control who has access to your calendar and how much they are allowed to see and edit.

In an office setting, however, the most common way to share calendar information is through Microsoft Exchange Server. With Exchange, you can grant permission for others to view and edit your calendar, depending on the settings you specify.

The steps below all require Microsoft Exchange Server to implement.

Step-by-Step

Share Your Calendar with Someone Else

1. In the **Navigation Pane**, check the box beside the calendar that you wish to share with another person.

2. Click the **Share Calendar** button  in the **Share** group on the **Home** tab to open an invitation email message.

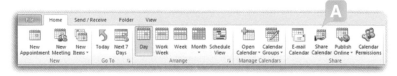

3. Enter the name of the recipient who you wish to share your calendar with in the **To...** line **B**.

4. Add any comments you want to the message body, then click **Send**. A message will be sent to the recipient informing them that you have shared your calendar.

5. Click **Yes**  in the **Share this Calendar...?** dialog box. The recipient will now be added to your permissions lists.

Step-by-Step

Set Permissions for Your Shared Calendar

1. Click the **Calendar Permissions** button **D** in the **Share** group on the **Home** tab to open the **Calendar Properties** dialog box.

2. Select the name of the person for whom you want to set new permissions **E**.

3. Select a permission level in the **Permission Level:** dropdown menu **F**:

   - **Owner** – Allows full access to the calendar. As an owner, you can create, read, modify, and delete all items in your calendar. You can also change settings for other people who have access to the calendar. It is recommended you not give other users this permission setting.

   - **Publishing Editor** – Contact can create, read, modify, and delete all items in your calendar. They can create and delete folders and subfolders.

   - **Editor** – Contact can create, read, modify, and delete all items and files, but cannot modify folders.

CONTINUE

- **Publishing Author** – Contact can create and read items and files, create subfolders, and modify and delete items that you create.

- **Author** – Create and read items and files, and modify and delete items that you create.

- **Reviewer** – Read items only.

- **Contributor** – Create items only.

- **Free/Busy time, subject, location** – Contact can view the time, the subject, and location of your appointments and meetings on your calendar.

- **Free/Busy time** – Contact can only see that you are free or busy. They cannot view any detail about your appointments.

- **Custom** – This designation will appear when you mark individual preferences by hand.

- **None** – Contact has no access to the calendar.

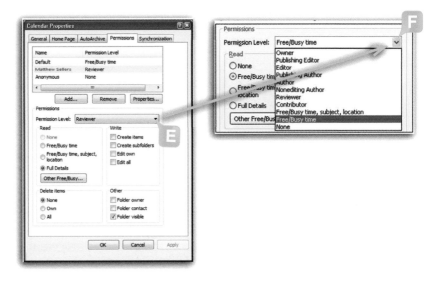

Each Permission Level represents a combination of permission settings that Outlook has pre-defined for you. Choose the level that is closest to the level you want. You can then edit the settings in the panes below. The Permission Level description will change to **Custom**.

In our Problem example above, your boss would need to share their calendar with you and then set your permission level to Publishing Author or a similar level.

Bright Idea: To ask someone to share their calendar with you, click on the **Open Calendar** button in the **Manage Calendar** group on the **Home** tab. Select **Open Shared Calendar** , then type in the name of the contact whose calendar you wish to view in the **Open a Shared Calendar** dialog box.

If the contact has already shared their calendar, it will open in your reading pane. If they have not shared their calendar with you, Outlook will prompt you to ask the person for permission. Click **Yes** and a sharing request email message will open. Click **Send** to send the request.

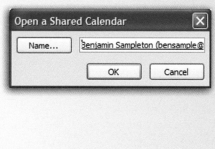

Hot Tip: If your manager needs you to not only view, add, and edit your calendar, but needs you to send email and invitations on his or her behalf, in a way that it seems the messages are coming directly from him or her, her or she will need to turn on **Delegate Access**. A delegate automatically receives Send on Behalf permissions, and can be granted extended permission up to and including Editor level permissions.

To turn on Delegate Permissions, click the **Delegate Access** menu option in the **Account Settings** dropdown menu on the **File** tab.

STOP

40 Categorize Items

Difficulty: ○○○○

PROBLEM You are managing multiple projects and want an easy way to categorize and organize emails, tasks, contacts, and calendar entries by project.

SOLUTION Assign Categories to each of your Microsoft Outlook items. Assigning categories allows you to group the items associated with each project, such as emails and tasks, into an easy-to-follow format in a single place. Because categories span all of Outlook's modules, your categories will be the same when you are organizing your emails as when you are assigning tasks.

Step-by-Step

1. Open the Appointment **A**, Task **B**, Message **C**, or Contact **D** that you want to assign to a category.

2. Click the **Categorize** button in the **Tags** group.

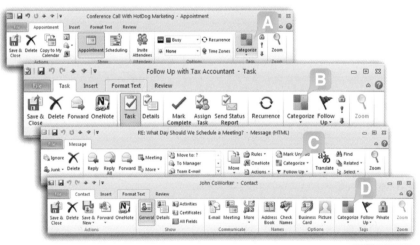

3. Select the category you want the item to be associated with from the dropdown menu **E**.

4. The category setting will be displayed in the appropriate manner for the Appointment **F**, Task **G**, Message **H**, or Contact **I** item.

Step-by-Step

Customize Categories

Outlook gives you a set of default color categories to get you started. The first time you use one of these defaults, Outlook will prompt you to customize the name of the category for future use. Type a new name for the category in the **Name:** text box

J to replace the default name. Assign a **Shortcut key:** if you wish from the dropdown menu **K**, then click **OK**.

1. To customize a category, click the **Customize** button in the **Tags** group, then select **All Categories** **L** from the dropdown menu to open the **Color Categories** dialog box.

2. To change the name of a category, select the color you want to change, then click the **Rename** button **M**. The name will become a text box **N**. Type your new name, then hit **ENTER**.

3. To change the color associated with a category, select the color you want to change, then choose a new color from the **Color:** dropdown menu **O**.

4. To set a shortcut key for a category, select the color you want a shortcut for, then choose one from the **Shortcut Key:** dropdown menu **P**.

5. To add a new category, click the **New…** button **Q**. Type a name for your new category, and select a color and **Shortcut Key**. Click **OK**.

6. Click **OK** to close the **Color Categories** dialog box when you have finished making your changes.

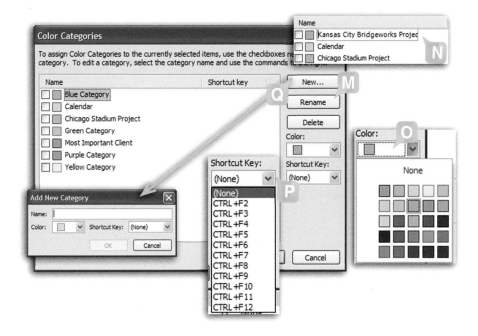

Quickest Click: Right-click on any item and choose the **Categories** option from the fly-out menu to assign a color category from the reading pane. Similarly, you can right-click on the **Category** column of a multi-column view to select a color category from the fly-out menu.

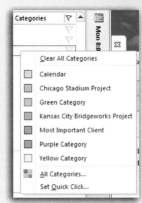

Hot Tip: If you frequently categorize email messages to the same category, you can set a default Quick Click category. Click the **Categorize** button in the **Tags** group, then select **Set Quick Click** . Choose a category for your quick click in the **Set Quick Click** dialog box , then click **OK**.

To assign the Quick Click category to an email message, simply click once in the **Categories Column** in the reading pane.

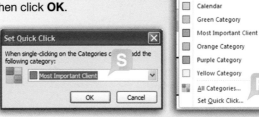

41 | Apply a Follow Up Flag to an Item

Difficulty: ⭕⭕⭕⭕

PROBLEM You are rushing out the door and don't have time to answer an email, but you want to make sure you don't forget to respond to the message later. You would like a quick way to mark the message so that it doesn't get lost among all the emails in your inbox.

SOLUTION Apply a **Follow Up** flag to an email message or contact that you don't want to forget. Use one of the default date categories or create your own. When a message or contact is flagged, the flag will appear in your email and contact (table) views next to the item. Follow Up flags will also appear in your To-Do Bar and in your Daily Task List to remind you to act upon the item.

Step-by-Step

1. Click the **Follow Up** button in the **Tags** group of an open email message **A** or contact **B** window.

2. Select the type of **Follow Up** flag you want to apply:
   - **Today** – The flag will assign a start and due date of the current date.
   - **Tomorrow** – The flag will assign a start and due date of the current date plus one day.
   - **This Week** – The flag will assign a due date of the last day of this week.
   - **Next Week** – The flag will assign a start date of the first work day of next week, and a due date of the last work day of next week.
   - **No Date** – The flag will not assign start or due dates.

- **Custom** – Choose your own start, due, and reminder dates.

3. To add a reminder to your item that already has a Flag, select it, then click the **Add Reminder** option from the **Follow Up** dropdown menu.

4. When you have set a **Follow Up** Flag, you will see the follow-up details in the item window on the information bar of your email message **D** or contact **E**. Your item will also appear in the To-Do Bar **F** and the Tasks View.

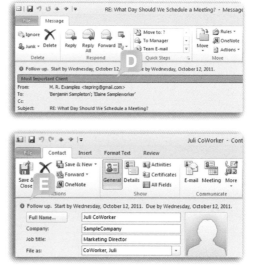

CONTINUE

Quickest Click: Right-click on a message or contact item and choose the **Follow Up** option from the fly-out menu to assign a **Follow Up** flag from the reading pane. Similarly, you can right-click on the **Flag status** column of a multi-column view to select a color category from the fly-out menu.

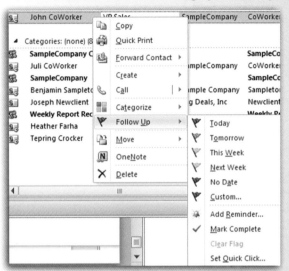

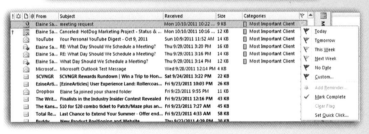

Hot Tip: If you frequently apply the same flag, such as Follow Up Tomorrow, you can set a default Quick Click Flag. Click the **Follow Up** button in the **Tags** group, then select **Set Quick Click** 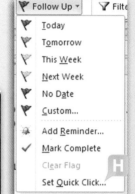. Choose a follow up flag for your quick click in the **Set Quick Click** dialog box , then click **OK**.

To assign the Quick Click Flag to an email message, simply click once in the **Flag Status Column** in the reading pane.

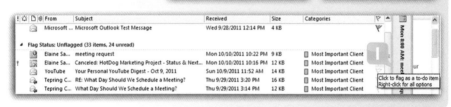

42 Mark an Item as Private

Difficulty: ◯◯◯◯

PROBLEM You share a calendar, tasks, and contacts with others in the office, and want to add your doctor's appointment and his contact information without everyone else seeing the details.

SOLUTION Enabling the Private function grants you the ability to hide any personal appointments or engagements on a calendar that may be shared. You can even choose to keep that appointment hidden on a printed copy of your calendar.

Step-by-Step

1. Select the Appointment **A**, Task **B**, or Meeting **C** in the Reading Pane, or open it in a window.

2. Click the **Private** button in the **Tags** group. The button will stay highlighted **D** to indicate that the item has been marked private.

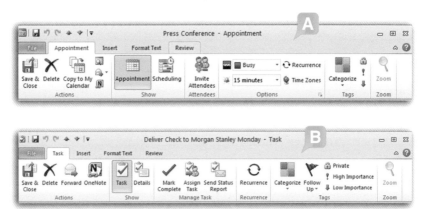

43 Archive Old Data with AutoArchive

Difficulty: ○○○○

PROBLEM You like to keep only the most recent information active in your Outlook folders. You would like a way to clean out and archive old information every six months without having to go through each item in all your folders.

SOLUTION The AutoArchive feature allows you to manage your mailbox or folders by moving older items to another location on your hard drive. Doing this will help to keep Microsoft Outlook clean and running quickly.

**Step-by-Step**

Set AutoArchive Preferences for All Folders

1. Click the **File** tab **A**, then click the **Options** button **B** to open the **Outlook Options** dialog box.

2. Click the **Advanced** button **C**.

3. Click the **AutoArchive Settings…** button **D** under the **AutoArchive** heading to open the **AutoArchive** dialog box.

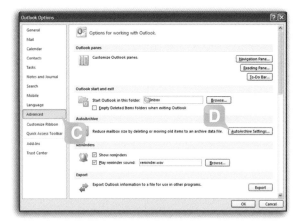

4. Click the **Run AutoArchive every ___ days** checkbox  to turn on **AutoArchive**. If it is not checked, AutoArchive will not run.

5. Enter the interval that you want between **AutoArchive** runs in the text box.

6. Under the **Default folder settings for archiving**, make a choice in the **Clean out items older than** dropdown menus to specify how old an item must be for it to be archived.

7. To move old items that **AutoArchive** will clean out into another folder (without deleting them permanently), click the **Move old items to:** radio button and specify the folder where they should go.

   To Permanently delete old items that **AutoArchive** will clean out, select the **Permanently delete old items** radio button.

8. Click **Apply these setting to all folders now** to run **AutoArchive**.

9. Click **OK** to close the **AutoArchive** dialog box and save your settings.

Step-by-Step

Set AutoArchive Preferences for a Single Folder

1. Right-click on any folder in the **Navigation Pane** and select **Properties** 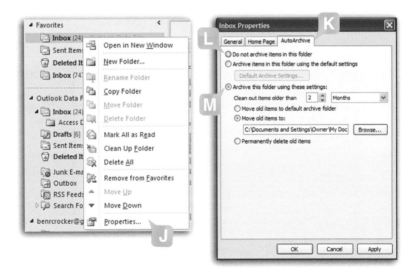 from the fly-out menu to open the **Folder Properties** dialog box.

2. Click on the **AutoArchive** tab.

3. Click the **Do not archive items in this folder** radio button to prevent **AutoArchive** from cleaning out the folder.

4. Click the **Archive this folder using these settings:** radio button to specify unique **AutoArchive** preferences for this folder.

5. Click **OK** to close the **Properties** dialog box and save your changes.

Caution: If you choose to have items deleted with the *permanently delete old items* option, your items will *not* be archived for future reference.

Clicking **Apply these settings to all folders now** will overwrite any unique **AutoArchive** settings you have made for individual folders.

44 | Create and Manage Rules

Difficulty: ○○○○

PROBLEM You receive a weekly trade publication via email. You like setting a time aside to read the latest news, but you don't like these emails filling up your inbox in the meantime. You would like a way to have them automatically moved to their own folder so they are also easier to find when you are ready to read them.

SOLUTION Create a Rule to automatically move your messages when they are received. Rules, either by using the default templates provided or by creating your own, automatically perform an action on your incoming or outgoing messages. With a rule, you can direct messages that meet your specific criteria to a specific location, apply a specific follow up flag or category, or even print it out. Creating a rule for your weekly trade publication will direct those documents to be moved to a folder of your choice automatically.

See Also: Send an Out-Of-Office Reply

Step-by-Step

Create a Rule Using an Outlook Template

1. Select the email message from the person or mailing list that you want to apply a rule to.

2. Click the **Rules** button  in the **Move** group.

3. Select **Always Move Messages From:**  from the dropdown menu to open the **Rules and Alerts** dialog box.

4. Open and select the folder you wish your messages to be moved to , or click the **New** button to create a new folder for your rule.

5. Click **OK** to save your rule. Outlook will run the rule against your current inbox and move all the existing messages that meet the rule into the folder you specified.

6. To edit or delete a rule, click on the **Rules** button in the **Move** group, then select **Manage Rules & Alerts** from the dropdown menu to open the **Rules and Alerts** dialog box.

7. Click on the rule you want to change, then make your changes from the menu bar.

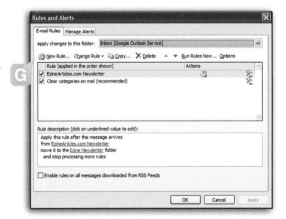

CONTINUE

Create and Manage Rules (continued)

Step-by-Step

Create a Rule Using an Outlook Template

1. Select the email message from the person or mailing list to which you want to apply a rule to.

2. Click the **Rules** button in the **Move** group.

3. Select **Create Rule...** H from the dropdown menu to open the **Create Rule** dialog box.

4. Select the conditions your rule must meet under the **When I get email with all of the selected conditions** heading I. You can choose one criteria, or more than one. The rule will apply only if all criteria are met.

5. Specify the action your rule will take when the criteria are met under the **Do the following** heading J. You can choose one or more actions.

6. Click **OK** to save and apply your rule.

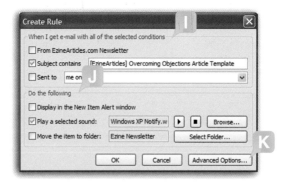

Hot Tip: For many more conditions and actions, click the **Advanced Options** button in the **Create Rule** dialog box. This will open the **Rules Wizard** to help you create complex and detailed rules.

45 Create and Manage Quick Steps

Difficulty: ○○○○

PROBLEM You are spending way too much time categorizing and moving email in your inbox.

SOLUTION Utilizing Quick Steps – simple, one-click buttons which perform multiple actions – will help you to save time by automatically filing your messages. For example, you could create a QuickStep allowing you to move all the emails from a specific client into the folder you have selected.

Outlook provides a default set of common Quick Steps for you to begin using right away. Some of these default Quick Steps will prompt you to configure them the first time you use them. They can then be customized, or you can create your own Quick Steps from scratch.

 Step-by-Step

---

Configure and Use Default Quick Steps

1. In the **Mail View**, select the email message in the reading pane that you want to act upon.

2. In the **Quick Steps** selection box, click the **Quick Step** action you want:

   - **Move to: ?** – Moves the selected message to the mail folder that you specify. The message will be marked as read.

   - **To Manager** – Forwards a copy of the message to your manager.

   - **Team Email** – Forwards the message to others in your team.

   - **Done** – Moves the message to a folder that you specify and marks the message as complete. The message will be marked as read.

   - **Reply & Delete** – Opens a reply window to the selected message and deletes the original.

   - **Create New** – Creates a new Quick Step.

3. The first time you use the **Move to: Team Email,** and **To Manager** Quick Steps, a **First Time Setup** dialog box will open. Fill out the information needed for the step, then click **Save** to close the dialog box and save your configurations.

4. To edit existing Quick Steps, click the **More** button **A** in the corner of the Quick Steps selection box.

5. Click the **Manage Quick Steps** menu option **B** to open the **Manage Quick Steps** dialog box.

6. Select the Quick Step you want to change in the **Quick Step** pane **C** to open its description in the **Description** pane.

7. Click **Edit D** to make changes, **Duplicate** to make a copy of the Quick Step, or **Delete** to delete the Quick Step.

8. Click the **Up** and **Down** arrows to move the Quick Step up and down in the selection box on the ribbon.

9. Click **OK** to close the dialog box and save your changes.

Step-by-Step

Create and Save a New Quick Step

1. Click the **More** button in the corner of the Quick Steps selection box.

2. Click the **New Quick Step** menu option , then choose the type of Quick Step you want to create from the fly-out menu to open the **First Time Setup** dialog box.

3. Fill out the criteria and actions for your Quick Step, then click **Finish**.

4. Your Quick Step will appear in the **Quick Step** selection box.

46 | Show in Favorites

Difficulty: ⦿○○○

PROBLEM You have many folders from past projects; however, you always seem to have a hard time finding the folder that contains the information for your current project.

SOLUTION Add the folder with the current information to the Favorites Folder. The Favorites folder always stays at the top of your Navigation Pane, making it easy to find. Under the Favorites folder, you can add, remove, and arrange sub-folders.

When a folder is added to Favorites, the original folder will remain at its original location in the folder list and a shortcut will be created. This ensures that your information stays organized, but gives you a way to put frequently-used content in an easier-to-use position. Similarly, removing the folder from Favorites does not delete the folder, but removes only the shortcut.

Step-by-Step

1. Click on the folder that you want to add to **Favorites**, then click the **Folder** tab A.

2. Click the **Show in Favorites** toggle button B in the **Favorites** group. The folder will appear under the **Favorites** heading in your **Navigation Pane** C. ⚡

3. To remove a folder from Favorites, select it, then click the **Show in Favorites** toggle button again.

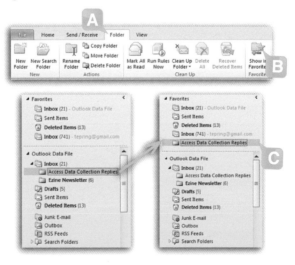

4. To rearrange the folders in Favorites, click and drag the folder to the position where you want it to appear. You can also click and drag folders from the original folder list directly into Favorites.

Quickest Click: Right-click any folder in the folder list, then select **Show in Favorites** 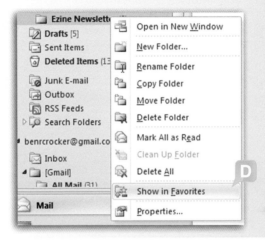 from the fly-out menu.

47 Search and Sort Your Email Messages

Difficulty: ◯◯◯◯

PROBLEM You know you recently received an email from your vendor with an updated proposal attached, but you can't seem to find it. And since you are having trouble finding things, you would like to clean out your inbox by grouping emails by sender, so you can move and delete messages in batches.

SOLUTION Outlook gives you many tools to organize and view your messages so you can find the ones you are looking for and manage your work efficiently. By adjusting your view, you can sort your messages in a number of ways, such as by date, category or priority. You can customize how messages appear, including specifying the order of the messages and the number of messages shown. When you know something about a message, such as whom it was from or a keyword in the subject line, you can search your inbox.

Step-by-Step

Search for Messages

1. In the **Mail View**, type a keyword or name into the **Search** box above the reading pane **A**.

2. As you type your keyword or name, Outlook will offer you an option to filter your search by **Keyword** (default), **From:**, or **To:** to help you quickly narrow your results **B**. Choose **From:** or **To:** when you want your keyword to only match a word in the From line or To line of the message.

3. When the reading pane is displaying a search result, the search bar will turn orange. Words that match your search term will be highlighted **C**.

4. Click the Search **Close** button **D** when you are done reviewing your search results.

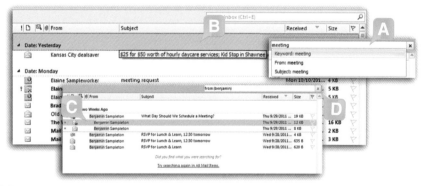

Step-by-Step

Sort and Group Your Messages

1. Click the **View** tab, then click the **More** button  in the corner of the **Arrangement** selection box in the **Arrangement** group.

2. Choose from the sorting options in the **Arrangements** selection box:

    *   **Date (Conversations)** – Groups messages with the same subject and in the same conversation together.

    *   **From** – Groups messages by sender.

    *   **To** – Groups messages by recipient.

    *   **Size** – Sorts messages by file size.

    *   **Subject** – Groups messages with the same subject, regardless of conversation.

    *   **Type** – Sorts by type of message such as Meeting Requests, Task Requests, Replies, etc.

    *   **Attachments** – Sorts by messages that contain an attachment.

    *   **Account** – Groups messages by the email account they are associated with.

    *   **Importance** – Sort your tasks by priority setting.

    Click the **Show in Groups** toggle 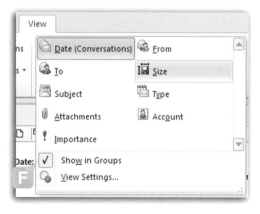 to group your tasks visually by the criteria you have specified.

CONTINUE

Quickest Click: You can easily sort your view by column simply by clicking on the column's heading **G**. Click a second time to reverse the sort **H**. A sort arrow will appear in the column, indicating the sort direction **I**.

Original

Sort by Subject

Sort by Subject Reversed

Hot Tip: You can customize your views even further from the **Advanced View Settings** dialog box. Select or arrange the view that is closest to what you are looking for, then click the **View Settings** button . In the dialog box, you can pick which columns you want and the order in which they appear . You can filter items and specify multiple sort orders (Sort by Date, then Priority, then Subject, for example.) Once you have created the view you need, click **OK** to apply the settings.

48 Set Up Your Outlook Window Layout

Difficulty: ○○○○

PROBLEM You spend a lot of time in Outlook every day, managing your tasks, appointments, and email messages. To save time, you would like to view your tasks and calendar along with your email inbox instead of switching between the views.

SOLUTION Change the Layout. By changing the default Layout, you can arrange the main Outlook window to display only certain items or display additional items such as tasks and calendars along with your email inbox.

See Also: Outlook Social Connector

 Step-by-Step

1. Click the **View** tab ⒜.

2. Click the **Navigation Pane** button ⒝ to view options for the placement and size of the Navigation Pane:

   • **Normal** – Will place your Navigation Pane on the left of your window with folders displayed.

   • **Minimized** – Will place your Navigation Pane on the left of your window in a narrow format.

   • **Off** – Will hide the Navigation Pane from your window.

   • **Favorites** – Will toggle the Favorites folder on or off of the Navigation Pane

3. Click the **Reading Pane** button ⒞ to view options for the placement and size of the Reading Pane. You can choose to place the reading pane on the right or bottom edge of your window, or hide it from your window.

4. Click the **To-Do Bar** button ⒟ to view options for the placement and features that will appear in your To-Do Bar:

   • **Normal** – Will place your To-Do Bar on the right of your window with folders displayed.

   • **Minimized** – Will place your To-Do Bar on the right of your window in a narrow format.

   • **Off** – Will hide the To-Do Bar from your window.

- **Date Navigator** – Will toggle the Calendar on and off of the To-Do Bar.
- **Appointments** – Will toggle Appointments on and off of the To-Do Bar.
- **Task List** – Will toggle Tasks on and off of the To-Do Bar.

5. Click the **People Pane** button 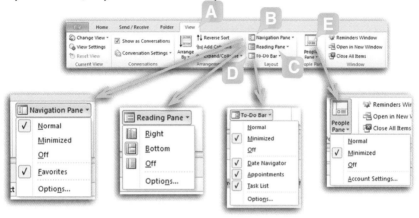 to view options for the placement and size of the People Pane. You can choose a **Normal** or **Minimized** pane at bottom edge of your window, or you can hide it from your window.

 Hot Tip: Once you have your panes organized, you can adjust the sizes of the panes to fit your personal workstyle. Put your cursor on the line where two panes meet. When the cursor turns into a double arrow 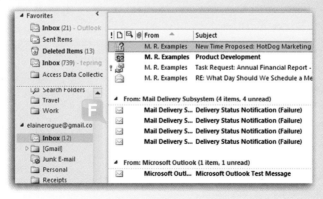, click then drag the border to the position you want it.

Customize Your Outlook Environment

Step-by-Step

Set User Preferences in Outlook

1. Click the **File** tab.

2. Click the **Options** button  to launch the **Outlook Options** dialog box.

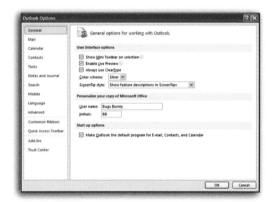

3. Click the menu tabs to view the options you want to adjust .

   General: Change some basic defaults within Outlook, including User Interface Options and Personalize Your Copy of Microsoft Office.

   Mail, Calendar, Contacts, Tasks, Notes and Journal: Customize features and appearance for the specific Outlook View.

   Search: Changed how Instant Search indexes and searches your items.

   Mobile: Customize and change settings for how items are sent to a mobile device.

Language: Choose your Office language preferences for proofing (spelling and grammar) and Help texts.

Advanced: Additional settings options for features such as reminders, RSS feeds, Dial-up connections, send and receive preferences, and international options.

Customize Ribbon: Add/remove and group items on the Ribbon.

Quick Access Toolbar: Add/remove items to/from the **Quick Access Toolbar.**

Add-Ins: Manage your Outlook **Add-Ins.** Note that most installed **Add-Ins** will not appear on the **Add-Ins** tab unless they are active.

Trust Center: Manage document security settings.

4.   Click the **OK** button.

B | Customize the Ribbon

Office 2010 introduced the ability to customize ribbon commands to a much greater degree. In 2010, you can create custom tabs and groups, rename and change the order of default tabs and groups, and hide both custom and default tabs.

To access the Customize options, click on the **File** tab, then click the **Options** button. This will launch the **Outlook Options** dialog box. Click on the **Customize Ribbon** tab .

Step-by-Step

Customize Tabs

1. To add a new tab to the Ribbon, click the **New Tab** button B under the **Customize the Ribbon:** window, in the **Outlook Options** dialog box. A new tab with the name **New Tab (Custom)** C will appear in the list.

2. Select the new tab and click the **Rename** button D. Type your custom tab name in the **Rename** dialog box E.

3. Click the **OK** button.

4. To move your new tab up and down on the list (or right and left on the Ribbon), select it, then click the up/down arrows to the right of the window **F**.

5. To hide a tab from being displayed on the ribbon, click the checkbox to the left of each tab **G** to uncheck it. Click again to unhide the tab and have it displayed in the Ribbon.

6. If you decide to remove a custom tab, right-click the tab in the **Customize the Ribbon:** list, then select **Remove** **H**. **Note:** You can hide, but you cannot remove default tabs.

Step-by-Step

Customize Groups

1. Click the **Expand** button ▮ to the right of any tab to view the groups that appear on the tab.

2. To add a new group to any tab, select the tab you want the group to appear on, then click the **New Group** button ▮ under the **Customize the Ribbon:** window. A new group with the name **New Group (Custom)** ▮ will appear in the list.

3. Right-click on the new group and select the **Rename** menu option ▮ to open the **Rename** dialog box.

4. Type your custom group name in the **Display name:** text box ▮. You can also select an icon to represent your custom group by clicking on any image in the **Symbol:** selection box ▮.

5. Click the **OK** button.

6. To move your new group up and down on the list (or right and left on the tab), select it, then click the up/down arrows to the right of the **Customize the Ribbon:** list.

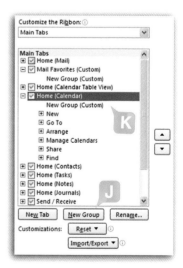

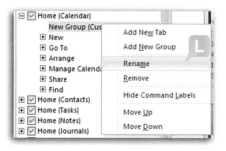

7. If you decide to remove a group from a tab, right-click the group in the
Customize the Ribbon: list, then select **Remove –OR–** select the group, then
click the **Remove** button between the **Choose** and **Customize** windows.

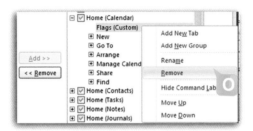

Step-by-Step

Add Commands to a Custom Group

1. Commands can only be added to custom groups, so begin by following the steps in the Customize Groups section to create a group for your commands.

2. Click on the command you want to add **P** in the **Choose commands from:** window.

3. Click on the destination custom group **Q**.

4. Click the **Add** button **R**. Repeat as needed.

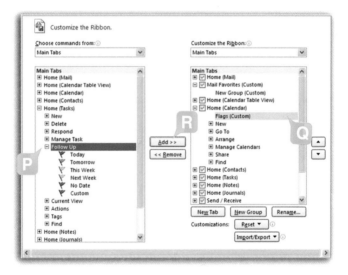

5. The command will appear under your custom group in the **Customize the Ribbon:** list.

6. To rename a command that you have added to a custom group, right-click on the command and select the **Rename** menu option. Type your command name in the **Rename** dialog box. You can also select an icon to represent your custom group by clicking on any image in the **Symbol:** selection box.

7. To move a command up and down on the list, select it, then click the up/down arrows to the right of the window.

8. If you decide to remove a command from your custom group, right-click the group in the **Customize the Ribbon:** list, then select **Remove** –OR– select the group, then click the **Remove** button between the **Choose** and **Customize** windows.

   Note: You cannot remove commands from default groups, although you can remove entire groups from tabs.

9. When you have made all your changes, click **OK** in the **Outlook Options** dialog box to save your settings and return to Outlook. Review your customized tab.

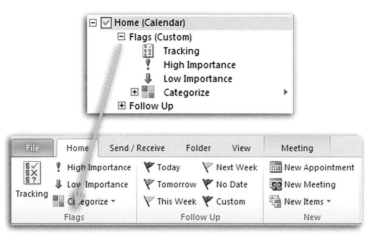

 Quickest Click: Right-click any item in the **Customize the Ribbon:** window for shortcuts to add new tabs or groups, show or hide tabs, and move tabs up or down.

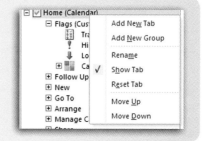

C | Keyboard Shortcuts

Keyboard Shortcut	Description
Common Tasks	
CTRL+A	Select All (effect depends on the tab you are working in)
CTRL+C	Copy selected text or object
CTRL+X	Cut selected text or object to the Office Clipboard
CTRL+V	Paste text or an object
CTRL+ALT+V	Paste special
CTRL+SHIFT+V	Paste formatting only
CTRL+Z	Undo the last action
CTRL+Y	Redo the last action

Create Items Shortcuts	
These commands work from any view	
CTRL+SHIFT+A	Create an appointment
CTRL+SHIFT+C	Create a contact
CTRL+SHIFT+L	Create a Contact List
CTRL+SHIFT+X	Create a fax
CTRL+SHIFT+E	Create a folder
CTRL+SHIFT+J	Create a Journal entry
CTRL+SHIFT+Q	Create a meeting request
CTRL+SHIFT+M	Create a message
CTRL+SHIFT+N	Create a note
CTRL+SHIFT+K	Create a task
CTRL+SHIFT+U	Create a task request

Editing Shortcuts	
Cursor needs to be inside a text box for these shortcuts	
ALT+O	Display the Format menu
CTRL+SHIFT+P	Display the Font dialog box
CTRL+B	Bold text
CTRL+I	Italic text
CTRL+U	Underline text
CTRL+SHIFT+< or CTRL+[	Shrink font size one increment
CTRL+SHIFT+> or CTRL+]	Grow font size one increment
BACKSPACE	Delete one character to the left
CTRL+BACKSPACE	Delete one word to the left

DELETE	Delete one character to the right
CTRL+DELETE	Delete one word to the right
CTRL+T	Increase indent
CTRL+SHIFT+T	Decrease indent
CTRL+K	Insert hyperlink
SHIFT+RIGHT ARROW	Select one character to the right
SHIFT+LEFT ARROW	Select one character to the left
CTRL+SHIFT+RIGHT ARROW	Select to the end of a word
CTRL+SHIFT+LEFT ARROW	Select to the beginning of a word
CTRL+A	Select all text in the text box
CTRL+E	Center paragraph
CTRL+J	Justify paragraph
CTRL+L	Left align paragraph
CTRL+R	Right align paragraph
CTRL+Q	Remove paragraph or character formatting

Moving Around Outlook

CTRL+1	Switch to Mail
CTRL+2	Switch to Calendar
CTRL+3	Switch to Contacts
CTRL+4	Switch to Tasks
CTRL+5	Switch to Notes
CTRL+6	Switch to Folder List in Navigation Pane
CTRL+7	Switch to Shortcuts
CTRL+PERIOD	Switch to next message (with message open)
CTRL+COMMA	Switch to previous message (with message open)
CTRL+1	Switch to Mail
CTRL+2	Switch to Calendar
CTRL+3	Switch to Contacts
CTRL+4	Switch to Tasks
CTRL+5	Switch to Notes
CTRL+6	Switch to Folder List in Navigation Pane
CTRL+7	Switch to Shortcuts
CTRL+PERIOD	Switch to next message (with message open)
CTRL+COMMA	Switch to previous message (with message open)

Mail View Shortcuts
These commands function as follows *ONLY* in the Mail View

CTRL+K	Check names
ALT+S	Send
CTRL+R	Reply to a message
CTRL+SHIFT+R	Reply all to a message
CTRL+ALT+R	Reply with meeting request
CTRL+F	Forward message
CTRL+ ALT+J	Mark message as not junk
CTRL+SHIFT+I	Display blocked external content (in a message)
CTRL+M or F9	Check for new messages
UP ARROW	Go to previous message
DOWN ARROW	Go to the next message
CTRL+N	Create a message (when in Mail)
CTRL+SHIFT+M	Create a message (from any Outlook view)
CTRL+O	Open a received message
CTRL+SHIFT+D	Delete and Ignore a Conversation
CTRL+SHIFT+B	Open the Address Book
CTRL+Q	Mark as read
CTRL+U	Mark as unread
CTRL+SHIFT+B	Open the Address Book
CTRL+ENTER	Send
CTRL+P	Print
CTRL+F	Forward
CTRL+ALT+F	Forward as attachment

Calendar View Shortcuts
These commands function as follows *ONLY* in the Calendar View

CTRL+N	Create an appointment (when in Calendar)
CTRL+SHIFT+A	Create an appointment (in any Outlook view)
CTRL+SHIFT+Q	Create a meeting request
CTRL+F	Forward an appointment or meeting
CTRL+R	Reply to a meeting request with a message
CTRL+G	Go to a date
ALT+= or CTRL+ALT+4	Switch to Month view

CTRL+RIGHT ARROW	Go to next day
ALT+DOWN ARROW	Go to next week
ALT+PAGE DOWN	Go to next month
CTRL+LEFT ARROW	Go to previous day
ALT+UP ARROW	Go to previous week
ALT+PAGE UP	Go to previous month
ALT+HOME	Go to start of the week
ALT+END	Go to end of the week
ALT+MINUS SIGN or CTRL+ALT+3	Switch to Full Week view
CTRL+ALT+2	Switch to Work Week view
CTRL+COMMA or CTRL+SHIFT+COMMA	Go to previous appointment
CTRL+PERIOD or CTRL+SHIFT+PERIOD	Go to next appointment
CTRL+G	Set up recurrence for an open appointment or meeting

Contacts View Shortcuts
These commands function as follows *ONLY* in the Contacts View

SHIFT+Letter	In the Card or Business Card view of contacts, go to the first contact that begins with a specific letter
CTRL+A	Select all contacts
CTRL+F	Create a message that uses the selected contact as subject
CTRL+J	Create a Journal entry for the selected contact
CTRL+N	Create a contact (when in Contacts)
CTRL+SHIFT+C	Create a contact (from any Outlook view)
CTRL+O	Open a contact form that uses the selected contact
CTRL+SHIFT+L	Create a Contact List
CTRL+P	Print
CTRL+SHIFT+B	Open the Address Book
CTRL+,	Go to previous message
ESC	Close a contact
CTRL+SHIFT+X	Send a fax to the selected contact
ALT+D	Open the Check Address dialog box
CTRL+SHIFT+ALT+U	Create a task request
INSERT	Flag an item or mark complete

Tasks View Shortcuts
These commands function as follows *ONLY* in the Tasks View

ALT+C	Accept a task request
ALT+D	Decline a task request
CTRL+E	Find a task or other item
CTRL+Y	Open the Go to Folder dialog box
CTRL+N	Create a task (when in Tasks)
CTRL+SHIFT+K	Create a task (from any Outlook view)
CTRL+O	Open selected item
CTRL+P	Print selected item
CTRL+A	Select all items
CTRL+D	Delete selected item
CTRL+F	Forward a task as an attachment
CTRL+SHIFT+ALT+U	Create a task request
INSERT	Flag an item or mark complete

The "Magic" ALT Key

When you press the ALT key on your keyboard, letters appear on the ribbon. Clicking a letter launches the corresponding function. Unlike other keyboard shortcuts, ALT shortcut keys are pressed sequentially, not held down at once. This can be much faster than using the mouse.

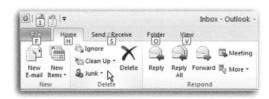

STOP